# SURVIVING SIXTEEN

Tina Prima Knaps

Copyright © 2024

All rights reserved.

# Dedication

*To anyone struggling, I know the struggle is real. Treatment, therapy, appropriate medication if needed, and time can heal. I was the one who had it all and still did not want to exist. I am very grateful to all of those who stubbornly insisted I listen to the words that I am now able to speak.*

*This is dedicated to all of those who never gave up on me. I am grateful to you all. It took me many years to know who I am and to be truly happy. I am so grateful. Sorry for any scars I created. My wish is that they have helped you grow in some positive way, but mostly, I hope they have healed.*

*Love Always,*

*Tina*

# Forward

Tina Knaps and I originally met as she was the head coach of my daughter's club volleyball team many years ago. As one can imagine, Ms. Knaps had a lot to manage other than just volleyball, as the coach of a dozen teenage girls who traveled across the country. Teenagers also have a lot on their plate with school, domestic, social responsibilities and commitments to name just a few. These responsibilities, expectations and commitments can become overwhelming lending to self-doubt and low self-esteem which without proper support and help can further develop into depression.

During the years of traveling to different tournaments Ms. Knaps and I learned more about each other's background including we both graduated from Tulane University (I quite a few years before her), her experience as a college athlete, and mine as a child and adolescent psychiatrist. The fact that I was a psychiatrist, Ms. Knaps felt comfortable discussing her history of depression in high school and college including the struggles and road blocks she faced and attempted to work through. The experience Ms. Knaps had with depression, in accompaniment with her years of coaching volleyball left such an impression that she felt compelled to write the book "Surviving Sixteen." "Surviving Sixteen" is a book in which multiple teenagers in first person format describe their daily struggles with depression and allows the reader to feel the emotions that these young adults try to navigate daily hoping to just make it till tomorrow. "Surviving Sixteen" is a book recommended for parents, guardians, school counselors and mature teenagers. The opportunity for open discussion/dialogue regarding feelings/struggles which occur on a daily basis is so important. The realization that one is not alone and that help is available is invaluable.

"Surviving Sixteen" opens a window for parents and guardians to see what their children are possibly experiencing while reminding parents of how they felt during these times of uncertainty and insecurity to again create the opportunity of conversation and non-judgmental dialogue. The topic of teenage depression for many may be taboo, overlooked, misinterpreted, minimized or even dismissed, which can only lead to greater and possibly tragic consequences. "Surviving Sixteen" may enlighten the reader to the signs, symptoms, of depression with the realization that with depression there is no one size fits all. Depression knows no socioeconomic, racial or ethnic background and as the book reveals it can affect all households despite what one thinks they see. The suicide rate for teenagers continues to rise with the key to reducing these numbers being earlier and better recognition of the symptoms of teenage depression. "Surviving Sixteen" helps educate the public in just this area and therefore helps to alert one to have greater awareness of changes in behavior to then start the process of seeking help.

Ms. Knap's personal experience along with her desire to help others has allowed her to write a book that will help those with depression to realize they are not alone and with the support of others feel comfortable seeking out and starting the treatment process they so desperately need and deserve.

*William Colomb MD*

*Child/Adolescent Psychiatrist*

# Acknowledgement

I would first like to thank my wonderful husband, Kenny Knaps, for his patience while I wrote this book. I ventured to some dark places that made it emotional and difficult for me, and therefore, I am sure, difficult for him too. Thanks to my talented daughter, Rachael Knaps, who so wonderfully voiced the audiobook version.

I appreciate all my family and friends whom I used as my beta readers. Thank you so much for your valuable feedback, Lynn Armstrong, Karen Cockerham, Sarah Cusimano, Dr. Patrick Glynn, Nancy Heck, Lisa Hidalgo, Julia Kemp, Margaret McCarthy, Roxanne Patti, Leah Peno, Charmaine Schneider, and Jackie Zeller. Thanks also to Becky Wilson, who took me under her wing and helped me polish my work.

I owe a debt of gratitude to my friend, Dr. William Colomb, who gladly read the book to ensure that I was dealing with the subject matter responsibly. Thank you for your kind words and the wonderful work you do with children and adolescents.

Everyone's unwavering support gave me the confidence to publish Surviving Sixteen and one last big thank you to all of you who helped me survive sixteen!

# Table of Contents

Dedication ..................................................................................... i

Forward ........................................................................................ iii

Acknowledgement ....................................................................... vi

Chapter 1 Nadia ........................................................................... 1

Chapter 2 Katrina ........................................................................ 15

Chapter 3 Reflections .................................................................. 27

Chapter 4 Homecoming .............................................................. 36

Chapter 5 Reality ......................................................................... 48

Chapter 6 Dominic ...................................................................... 57

Chapter 7 The Sassos .................................................................. 70

Chapter 8 Do ................................................................................ 81

Chapter 9 Aidan .......................................................................... 92

Chapter 10 Youth On Fire .......................................................... 103

Chapter 11 Opportunities .......................................................... 116

Chapter 12 Missed Opportunities ............................................. 129

Chapter 13 911 ............................................................................ 145

Chapter 14 Outreach .................................................................. 152

Chapter 15 Angel's Plea ................................................................. 159

Chapter 16 Diana ........................................................................ 168

Chapter 17 The Letters ............................................................... 181

About The Author....................................................................... 185

Mental Health Resources ........................................................... 186

Pact For Survival ........................................................................ 188

Letter Of Commitment To Ask For Help Before Harming Oneself................................................................................... 189

# Chapter 1
# Nadia

That repetitive creaking of the bed in the room next door, the release of satisfaction that can only be brought on by one thing, then a giggle or two, gross! Why are my parents so in love? And don't they know that I now realize they are not "wrestling" like they claimed when I was a kid and would want to join in? Ugh...gross! When are they going to grow up and grow apart like most parents do?

No, I need to have the perfect family, happily married parents who are still in love and still having sex, making love, uh, sounds terrible no matter how you say it...gross! The Baxter family has one girl, one boy, a dog named Spot, and a house on the hilltop. How freaking perfect! What more could a girl want?

How about parents who don't check your phone, room, or grades? I don't want to partake in family dinner at least five nights a week! Some of my friends don't even eat dinner five nights a week, much less with both or even one of their parents. Suzy doesn't even know who her dad is, for all we know, he could be the guy she went out with the other night. He was old enough. He treated her to dinner and then had her for dessert at the Ole Ye Hotel Motel.

Oh man, wait till I tell her that theory. She'll die. Lol.

Surviving Sixteen

I stir around in my bed, trying to make myself get up. Phrases rattle off in my head, "Get up, let's go make the best of the day, take the bull by the horns, and use your time wisely." I have heard them all. My mom is the best at reminding me of these so-called words of wisdom.

I drag my weary body out of bed. Why does high school start so early? You know studies have shown that we teenagers need our sleep. Whatever...it won't change. Why try to reason with adults? We just have to follow the rules, do what we're told or there will be consequences.

"Can't get away with stuff like that in the real world," says every adult ever.

Hello...I believe I am in the real world. What would you call this? Hell? For example, school starts so early. I mean, it's so dumb. Oh, and guess what? If you can't make it on time, there are consequences. Three tardies, yeah, that's a Saturday detention. How stupid. If you can't make it on time during the week, what makes them think you want to get up on a Saturday? Don't talk to me about the real world. I'm already living it.

I step into the warm running water of the shower, lay my head back, and feel the warmth of the water in my hair. It fills my head, my neck, and my breasts and glides down my stomach and legs, bringing a great sensation all the way to my toes. I lather my hair with a new shampoo that my mother recently purchased. It is refreshing, and the smell suddenly brings me back to our cruise to the Caribbean.

The ship was so luxurious, with live music, shows, and daily and nightly activities, delicious food and all the ice cream you could want. Relaxing in the pool, all the while eye-balling the guys diving into the crystal-clear water or as their bodies shimmer while shooting basketball at the nearby court.

My sunscreen! That's what it smells like. The coconut and lavender blend bring back reminders of such a great time. Too bad it was so long ago. I could use a vacation now. School has me so stressed. I lay my head back in the shower and wash away the shampoo and the memories. It all goes down the drain. Perfect metaphor. That's how I feel my life is going lately.

I get ready for school, dressing in the clothes I so carefully picked out the night before, a cute skater skirt and bright flowing top, accessories, and ankle boots and I am ready to take over Stratford High. I grab breakfast my mom has fixed for me and call for my little brother to come on. I don't know why Mom or Dad can't take him to school on the way to work. He is their son, but no... "Nadia Baxter, if you want a car, you must start taking on some responsibilities."

"Let's go, Dweeb!" I yell and walk out the door. In all honesty, I don't mind bringing him. It is on my way and he is a pretty good kid. He is in second grade. His name is Dominic, but I call him Dom, Little Man, and his least favorite name, Dweeb.

"Why do you always call me that?" he calls out and runs behind me to catch up.

On the way to school, Dom and I jam out to my favorite music, play Punch Buggy, and just enjoy each other's company. Actually, this is the only time I really like spending with him. Otherwise, he is always in the way, wanting something, barging into my room, and getting everything he wants from my parents. He is so spoiled, but something about it, being just the two of us, listening to music and playing games, makes the rest of the world disappear for a short while.

"We're here. Come on, Dweeb. Get out. I gotta go."

"Don't call me that," he replies as he gets his backpack on and leaves.

"Hey Dom," I call out to him, "have a good day, Little Man."

He turns and looks at me with his big, goofy smile.

"You too," he said.

After I drop him off at his school, I head to my school. I get my thoughts together for the day. You have to be on top of your game, or you could get eaten alive or just disappear. High school is tough. Only the strong survive. You have to know everyone and be able to size them up quickly, otherwise you lose the advantage.

People say that I am popular, but others label me a mean girl. But if I am so mean, then why am I popular? It's not that I am mean, people are just jealous, and there is nothing I can do about that. I just live my life and try to be happy. It's not like I can change my looks, intelligence, or attitude. Sure, I could try. I could not brush my hair, wear makeup, or pretend to be dumb, but that is not who I am. I can't help it if all the guys want me and all the girls want to be me.

People think it's easy to be me, but it's tough to have so much pressure. Every now and then, someone pretends they don't care what I think, and I have to put them in their place in front of everyone. Talk about pressure, teachers, counselors, etcetera, call me into their office and tell me what a role model I am and how I should be "gentle" with the less popular kids.

They have no clue! I am trying to help keep myself on top and keep the less popular kids from committing total social suicide. I am the youngest in my class because my parents made me skip a year, yet I am still at the top of my class, and I am not about to let that change: 4.0 GPA, President of the Senior Class, and a star athlete. What more could a girl want, right?

Jacob Domiano! That's what! He is the hottest guy in school. Boy, did he develop over the summer? I think I might love or at least lust him. My friend just told me that he will ask me out, he and I, Homecoming King and Queen. It will be a great finishing touch to my high school career. This is my senior year and things couldn't be better, right?

That's what it appears like to everyone looking in, but things could be better. It is as if I am constantly surrounded by a fog, a dirty gloomy fog. If I am talking with friends or playing ball, then the air movement I create clears my way. But if I am still and thoughtful, it closes in on me and threatens to darken by the minute. I try to keep busy. As I said, if I am busy, the wind created by my movement helps lift the fog, but I'm tired. I sometimes just want to be still, but being still with my thoughts, it's terrifying, so instead, I continue to move and be happy for all the world to see.

Made it to school, hopped out, thinking, what have I got to lose? I enjoy being with my friends, and classes are okay, although I would never admit it.

"Suzy," I call out to my friend as I get out of my car. "Guess what I thought about? Remember that guy you hooked up with? He is old enough to be your dad. What if he actually is?"

We both gag a little, then laugh all the way to class.

English is first period; our graded reports are being handed out to us. I get mine. "Wonderful!!!" That's what is written on my paper, along with an A+. Everyone else is complaining about their grades. I put mine away and go along with the rest of the class.

"Wonderful!!!" That's it? It seems so blah! It's the grade I always get, not deserve, but get. If the teacher only knew the effort I put into this paper was minimal. Can't you challenge me? Isn't there something I could improve on? What was the strongest point? What was the weakest part? I know I can't talk to anyone about this because they wouldn't understand. They would kill for my grades. I should be happy. I am wonderful!

"You are so smart."

"I wish I had your grades."

"You should be proud of yourself."

These are all things I hear often, but I cannot shake the fog closing in, wondering if this is as good as it gets. I sure don't feel wonderful.

I make it through to lunch and sit with my friends. Suzy, Nadia, that's me, Annie, and Paulette, "SNAP" that's what we call ourselves. We always sit together. We've been friends since middle school. We vowed to stay together and rule high school. I'd say we have succeeded. SNAP to it. Whatever we want, we get, SNAP, it's done. It's nice being on top.

I now have to make the big decision for the day: what to eat. There is a salad bar in our cafeteria. That is what I usually eat, but today is my favorite, Taco Tuesday. I decided to splurge and get the tacos. Tacos on corn shells with a side of corn, I'll never get cafeteria food. I eat the tacos, skip the corn, and drink the bag of skim milk. Milk in a bag…so weird.

This just means I'll have to jog extra today. I cannot afford the extra calories. My mom is always on me about what I eat, that's her thing. I think she was overweight when she was young and didn't want me to go through what she did. She tells me her stories of the popular girls making fun of her and calling her "fatty." She said it wasn't until she started working out and getting in shape that she started looking and feeling better. That's about when she met Dad. Well, I am already thin, popular and fit, so I guess I have nowhere to go from here but down. Like I said, pressure.

At lunch, the big chatter is that there is a new girl in school. She just moved here from New Orleans. Her home was flooded in Hurricane Katrina, and she and her parents are living here with her grandmother. She will probably finish her senior year here with us. That really sucks for her. I would hate to change schools during my senior year, nonetheless, I move hundreds of miles away from my friends or hometown. The other thing that sucks is her name. It is Katrina! She told everyone it was Kat, but Mrs. Wild called her Katrina and made a big deal about how easy it would be to remember her name, Katrina, like the storm Hurricane Katrina that brought her here. I think Mrs. Wild needs to be called into the office and taught how to be "gentle."

I get my tacos and sit down.

"Hey guys, look. There's Jacob's crew. Where's Jacob? I don't see him, is he not here today?"

"No," Suzy responds snidely. "He is just not sitting with them. Look behind you."

I turn around and see him sitting with someone I do not know. Apparently, it's the new girl, Kat. Wow, she is pretty, and she is eating a salad!

"Principal Tanner probably asked him to show her around. He is the President of the Student Council. That's what they do, right? It's his job," I assure myself.

"Ah, yeah, sure," all three friends reply together.

The bell rings, and we head to class. I go to science class, which would have been uneventful, except, halfway through, who comes in but Katrina, the new girl. I finally get a good look at her. Wow, she is beautiful!

I sure hope Jacob had to show her around, which is why they were together. What will I do if he chose to sit with her at lunch? The storm clouds are closing in. I can feel the darkness surrounding me and getting thicker by the minute. I do not know what I would do if Katrina stormed into my life and blew up my senior plans.

"Jacob's mine," I send a subliminal message for now, but I will upgrade it later if necessary.

"Well, hello, Katrina!" I call out. The movement of the air gives me some breathing room. Calling her Katrina instead of Kat gives me even more, chasing the smothering fog away. As I expect, Katrina just nods and sits down. I have nothing to worry about, I definitely have the upper hand.

Calculus class was the last class of the day. Jacob is in this class and we sit next to one another. I, needless to say, love partner work. We are both good at math, so we always finish our problems rather quickly and have time to chat. I use this time to flirt and can feel our connection growing closer and closer. Today, I will feel him out to see what he thinks about the new girl.

My plan is busted when, as soon as I get to class, I hear, "Clear your desks, pop quiz. I want to see how well you are understanding the lesson. I hope you did your homework."

Everyone grumbles and groans. I look at Jacob, and he looks at me. We smile at each other.

Dang it! No group work today.

After the last bell, there is a mass exodus from our school building. Almost everyone heads to their bus or cars to head home. My day is not finished yet, we have basketball practice. I am the quickest point guard Stratford High has ever had. I work hard at this; I am a good athlete and really enjoy playing.

The darkness I spoke of earlier has no place in the gym. It cannot get to me there even though our team isn't very good. Last year, we had an even season, winning 10 games and losing 10 games, and this year we are on the same pace. It doesn't matter to me. Well, it matters, I want to win.

I push myself and everyone to do their best and work hard, but even if we lose the darkness cannot get to me, not there. The only problem is that I can't stay, practice always ends. My coach lets me stay for extra shooting practice but eventually kicks me out.

Practice goes off without a hitch. I run, I jump, and the air lightens and brightens. I could stay here forever. We practice our man-on-man and zone defense. We do layups, give and go's, and three pointers. Swish, yes! I love that sound. The rest of the world fades away for a while.

Official practice ends and I stay to practice some extra shooting as usual.

"Let's go, Nadia. I have to lock up and get out of here," Coach Macy yells across the gym.

"Five more minutes?"

"OK, but that's it. I have a date tonight. Need to get home and get ready."

"Whoa…. WHAT!! Who is the lucky guy?"

"None of your business. Now get out."

"Oh, come on, Coach. You can't do that. Who is it? Where are you going? Is it serious? How long have you been seeing him?"

"Nadia, this is not something we are going to discuss and if you don't leave, I'll never make it, so get out!"

I grab my stuff and go. "Have fun on your date. Don't do anything I wouldn't do," I laugh as I leave.

I drive home with my mind racing. Coach Macy has a love life. Wow, I never really thought about her life outside of school or ball. I guess we all have things in our lives that no one realizes. Again, I guess people see what they want to see or what we allow them to see.

Like right now, a young, pretty girl is driving a cute car and singing along to the radio. Grownups look in and think or say, "I wish I were in high school again, with friends, dances, Friday night football, no bills, and no stress of a real job or a hard-ass boss." I don't know what high school was like back when they were in school, but there's plenty of stress, pressure, and hard-ass teachers. How could they forget so quickly?

Sometimes, it just seems like it's too much. Sometimes, I wonder why we are even here. Why do we even exist, and what if we didn't anymore? My mind starts to wander. Like, I mean, if you like it here and want to be here, then, great, you can be. But if you are tired and done, why can't you choose to stop existing, like, just go to sleep and fade away?

Hoooooonk!!!!! Screech! Aaahhh!! I slam on my brakes. I stop breathing for what feels like a lifetime as my car skids sideways. A dump truck flies past me. I was within a hair of being smashed by this humongous truck.

I totally blew through that stop sign. Oh my gosh! I am so sorry. I could have killed somebody. I could have killed myself. Breathe, just breathe. I drive the rest of the way home much more carefully, the fog closing in.

When I arrive home, Dweeb is waiting for me.

"Wanna play? I've been waiting for you."

"I can't, I have to study."

"Please, please, please, just for a little," he begs.

I run towards him in a playful manner, and he takes off. We play chase like this for a few minutes before I catch him, tackle and tickle him. He really is a great kid, and I notice that the fog has somewhat lifted. Dominic seems to have that superpower over me when I let my guard down. We play for a little longer before I go inside.

I head upstairs to my room and hit the books. Projects to work on, tests to prep for, essays to write, and college applications to fill out. It never seems to end. School, school, and more school, only to become an adult who wants to go back to being in high school...argh! What's it all about? I don't want to do this.

"Nad, it's dinner time. Come on down," my mom yells.

I don't want to do that either, I think to myself.

The talk at the dinner table is our normal family chatter. I really am blessed, I realize as I sit, watching my brother laugh with my mom and dad. I can't really complain about my life, which makes my situation even more depressing. Why can't I be happy? I really do have it all.

"May I be excused?"

"It's your turn to help with cleaning up," Mom reminds me.

"Not tonight, please," I kind of whine.

"It's your responsibility. We all must do our part, and tonight is your night."

"I just can't tonight, Mom. Please."

"I'll do it," Dominic comes to my rescue.

"No," Dad states firmly. "We all have to do things we don't want to do. It's part of life, Nadia, get to it."

I clam up because I know it's a losing battle. I clean up, making a little more noise than necessary, banging the pots and pans, and then head up to my room.

I go straight to the shower. No one can see your tears when you are showering. What is wrong with me? A fog fills the room. I wish it was steam from the shower, but it's not. It is the dark, dirty gloomy fog that seems to find me when I'm alone.

I cry.

# Chapter 2
# Katrina

I get a good night's sleep and wake up ready to go. I put my game face on, ready to seize the day. It's breakfast with the fam, Punch Buggy with Dom, and school with Jacob. Yes, Jacob Domiano is what I am missing in my life. I'm popular, have great grades, am good at sports, and have a nice car. Now, all I need is the guy of my dreams to make me happy.

"Lookout, Jacob, I choose you."

I meet up with Suzy and we walk into school and see something odd. A table is set up with a banner taped across it, "Are You Happy?"

"What's this?" Suzy asks.

"I don't know," I reply, "but it looks like Jacob is working on it. He can make me happy. Let's go see."

I freshen up my lipstick and strut over, catching Jacob's eye on the way.

"What's all this about? I know what will make me happy," I say with a flirty hint.

Just as I finish speaking, no one other than Katrina walks up and puts her hand on the small of Jacob's back! I tried not to react, but it was like gale-force winds just blew me over. What in the world is happening? This kind of thing did not happen to me. I just flirted with someone and he would now swoon over me. That's how my life works. This cannot be happening.

"School has allowed us to set this booth up. It's to help build up interest. A local church is putting together a mission for the summer. They will be sending people to New Orleans to help with the recovery from Hurricane Katrina," Jacob explains with a big smile on his face, a smile that is way too big to be brought on by some church mission.

"So why does the sign say…Are You Happy?" I ask him with an attitude because, yeah, now he is dumb.

"Well," Katrina intrudes, "true happiness can come from helping others. Often, this is the only time we find true meaning in life. God has created us to love each other."

"Isn't that nice? God tore up and flooded your home so that you could move hundreds of miles away and come to teach us how to live happy little lives. Wasn't that kind of Him?"

"Oh no, I'm devastated by what happened, but I want to take this opportunity to grow, and happiness will come from helping those less fortunate. In the Bible, Proverbs reminds us that 'Those who live to bless others will have blessings heaped upon them, and the one who pours out his life to pour out blessings will be saturated with favor.'"

"Yeah, well, the Lord helps those who help themselves too. So," I pause, "Good for you."

I turn and walk away with my head held high. No one is going to come here and tell me how to be happy or quote scripture to me. I am at the top of my class, 4.0 GPA, President of the Senior Class, and a star athlete.

I go through the rest of the day with a chip on my shoulder but a huge smile on my face. I am in rare form, showing off every chance I get.

To be quite honest, it is exhausting.

I leave school pretending to be at the top of my game, but when I get in my car, the fog sets in quickly. I'm tired. The darkness fills my thoughts. I just want to go home and sleep.

I pull up at my house, park, and look up. There's Dominic doing some funky little dance. He's always so happy. I wish I could be as carefree as him.

"Come, dance with me"

"I can't. I have to study."

"Please, please, please, just for a little," He begs.

"Not today!" I yell at him.

I don't want to play right now, I'm pissed. Just leave me alone. Why do you like me so much anyway? You little dweeb.

"Get lost. I already said no," I fuss at Dominic in a bitchy voice. I can even hear it. Why am I so freaking mean?

My thoughts are racing and spinning. My body hurts. Hurts? Well, just heavy, my body is heavy. It takes effort to move. I manage to make it upstairs, go to my room, close and lock the door.

My mom follows behind me and knocks, "You okay?"

"Yes," I answer, and if you all would just leave me alone, follows in my head.

"I'm just a little tired," I call out.

I could tell she was still outside my door, so I added, "I just have a little headache. Took some Tylenol, and I'm just going to rest."

"Okay," my mom replies and walks away. "Let me know if there is anything I can do," I hear her voice as it trails away.

Why can't she just leave me alone? My door is closed and locked. That does not mean, come bother me. God, I wish she would just leave me alone.

I fall asleep, and the next thing I hear is a soft knock on the door.

"It's dinner time. Don't you want to come eat?"

"Is my door open yet?" I whisper to myself. "No, it's not."

My bitch voice is still there. Couldn't sleep it away this time. Well, since my sleep was so rudely interrupted, I guess I am a little hungry. I get up and head down to dinner.

Sure enough, everyone is seated at the table. Family dinner, at least five nights a week. "A family that dines together shines together," a plaque hanging on the wall mocks me.

"So, how are you feeling?" my mom asks.

"I'm fine," I reply. "Guess I just needed to rest a little."

"Sorry, you're sick," says Dominic. "And I do the dishes tonight, so don't worry."

I look at him and, without much thought, roll my eyes. God, why is he always so nice to me? Why? I can be such a bitch. I eat for about five minutes.

"I'm finished. May I be excused? I have lots of homework to do tonight."

"Sure," my dad replies. He has been talking about his day but pauses to talk to me for a minute. "Don't stay up too late tonight. Get some sleep. Your mom tells me you are not feeling well."

"There's a virus going around out there. Do you have a fever, Sweetie?" Mom chimes in.

"No, Mom, and yes, sir. That's why I want to be excused. I plan to finish my work and go straight to bed early tonight. I have a big game later this week."

"Oh yeah," exclaims Dad. "It's always a close game when you all play Lincoln Academy. Those girls are so big."

"Tall like Lincoln. That's what we always say. What do they feed them over there?" I laugh, feeling better for a minute.

I get up, and the heaviness hits. I drag my body upstairs into the fog that awaits. I manage to get my homework done, shower, and go straight to bed.

"Great," I think to myself as a twist and turn. Now I can't sleep.

I pick up my phone and look at some posts. Do I dare look up Katrina? Yep. I type in Katrina and hesitate. What is her last name? I can't remember, but I hit enter as if the social media gods are going to magically know who I am talking about.

Oh my! The pictures that appeared on my screen are surreal. There are several pictures of New Orleans and the damage it has sustained from Hurricane Katrina. There were people sitting on their roofs. They had apparently gone up to the attic to get out of the flood waters and gotten stuck up there. As the water rose, desperation set in, and they had to bust a hole in their roof with an axe and escape to the rooftop. And there they sat, waiting to be rescued. Some people wait up there for hours, others days. Again, so surreal.

I begin scrolling through and see more vivid images. It seems like another country, a third world. More pictures of people trying to escape the flood waters. People huddled together on bridges, others walking in the water pushing their child who is sitting in a big plastic bin. The rain had stopped, yet the water kept rising because the levees had broken. They were stranded in muddy flood waters. Ironically, water all around them and yet, no water to drink.

"It's like hell on earth," I thought and "Wow, 'It took 5 days for FEMA to get drinking water to the Superdome, an evacuation center,'" I read a caption aloud.

I continue to look at pictures, read articles, and think of the horrors those people faced. Coffins had even been seen floating in the flood water. Can you imagine? And now, what now? I search more on Hurricane Katrina and see the damage that it left behind. There was a house that was now in the middle of an intersection, it had floated away.

I think of the new girl, Katrina, and wonder if that could be her house on the road or if she had to climb out of a hole cut in her roof. Did she see her relative's coffin floating down the street? I'm such a selfish bitch. I cry myself to sleep.

The days seem to drag on. I go to school, do my thing, you know, put on a happy face, be the perfect student, and then go home and do my thing there, wallowing in self-pity. At least I can put on a show at school, no one really notices a change. I am still the best. Jacob and Katrina are going steady, and they plan to save the world and make people happy by convincing them to join their club. There is no way that I want in. I have enough problems of my own.

Like I said, school is fine, I can turn it on, but once school lets out, I am done. I cannot keep up the charade, it's exhausting. My parents seem to notice my fatigue. I wonder if they can see the dark, gloomy fog that follows me around. It's kind of like that cartoon character from Charlie Brown. What's his name? Pig-Pen, although it's fog, not gross, stinky dirt.

My parents are getting worried. They think I am sick and make an appointment for me to see our doctor.

"Maybe she has Mono," I hear them talk.

Isn't that the kissing disease? How could I have mono when I don't have Jacob Domiano? Maybe I am sick. That may be a good thing. I can get some medicine, feel better, and get back to being my old self. What is that even? I don't know anymore. I just know who I am now, a fake, beautiful, happy-go-lucky, smart, popular girl to the world, yet a dark, gloomy, wet, limp rag once the show is over. I just know that I put on my game face and make it through the day. I do what I have to, but I don't really want to do anything.

Mom takes me to the doctor. He checks my eyes, ears, nose, and throat, I gag. I hate it when they stick that thing in my throat.

"Looks good. Have you had a sore throat lately?" the doctor asks.

"Ah, no. Well," I pause and think. "Yeah, I had a cold a couple of weeks ago. I was stopped up, and my throat hurt, but I'm better now."

"Well, everything looks good now, but I want to do some bloodwork."

"She has been so fatigued. Someone mentioned mononucleosis. Do you think it could be that?" my mom asks, she's always so worried.

"Let's wait on the results from the bloodwork, and we will go from there. There are many things that can cause such fatigue. We will get to the bottom of it."

The doctor looks at me and smiles.

"Yeah, Mom," I think, "just let him do his job. You always want to fix everything."

Mom and I leave the doctor. Just as I am getting more depressed and aggravated, my mom has the best idea.

"Want to go for ice cream?" she asks.

"What a crazy question! Of course, I do. I love ice cream."

A minute later, I'm aggravated again. Mom changes her mind. She pushes for frozen yogurt instead, supposed to be better for you. I agree to the frozen yogurt, but can't we just do something without so much thought? Ice cream that was what you said. Why did we have to rethink it and decide that frozen yogurt would be better? I want ice cream, but agree to frozen yogurt anyway, because that is what is expected of me. Make the wise choice, do the right thing. Suddenly, I feel sick again.

Mom calls Dad, and he and Dominic meet us there. I get a small chocolate with strawberry topping. We sit and visit. It's kinda nice. I finish my yogurt and put my head down for a minute, and fog continues creeping in.

I sit like that for a few minutes, and then I hear giggling and look up. Dominic has finished his yogurt and is up doing some little crazy dance that all the kids do. I wish I were still a kid like him, he is so carefree. Always makes me laugh. My dad gets up and mimics him.

"Oh no, please don't! Dad!" I call out. "You are so embarrassing."

I should not have said that, because now my mom joins in. All three of them are doing the floss. Oh my gosh. How embarrassing, yet fun, if I'm being honest. I fuss at them and tell them to stop, but as I get up, I floss a little myself. Not very obviously, but in a sly sort or sneaky way so the world can't see me. We all laugh. Dom literally starts rolling on the floor laughing.

"Get up!" we all yell. "The floor's dirty!"

"Ewe, gross. Come on, Little Man," I reach down and help him up. Ah, that was fun. I haven't laughed like that in a while.

We get home and keep up with family time. I don't mind; it's a nice distraction. We play board games, chat, and laugh. What a great evening!

The next few days, I seem to feel a little better, but not great. I still mope around at home, but school is getting a little easier. The doctor calls. He said that all my tests are negative and if the problem persists, it may be a good idea to see a counselor.

"It may be psychological. Depression can cause the symptoms you are describing," he explains to my mom. "If it doesn't get better, I'd like her to see a colleague of mine. She's a counselor who is great with teens."

What does that even mean? He wants me to see a counselor. No way, I have been feeling better and do not want to go to a shrink, absolutely not!

My mom doesn't make me go at first, but as time progresses, I get back into my sleeping routine. It was that stupid phone call, it got me thinking. The doctor thinks there is something wrong with me. He wants me to see a shrink? I know I'm not crazy, but the thought of it seems to make me crazy. I start feeling down again, kind of a heavy feeling. Just leave me alone. I like it here in my room, alone. That's all I really want to do, stay in my room with the door locked.

I mostly sleep; it is a great escape. When I sleep, no thoughts race through my head. I do not feel the dense, smothering fog that surrounds me. Sleep, that's the solution.

I hear my parents talking and know that they are going to make me go to counseling.

"All she does is lock herself in her room and sleep," I hear them whisper. "It's not good. We have to do something. Even Dominic is asking what's wrong with her and why won't she play with him."

"Great, a shrink. I don't think so. You can't make me. Y'all are so stupid. Just leave me alone." I bitch to myself. "Great," I think again, "even my thoughts are bitchy."

# Chapter 3
# Reflections

This is my new norm and I have no choice. It is either go to counseling and keep my car or lose my driving privileges. Really, what would you choose? You know you need that car. You could never go back to riding the school bus or having your parents bring you to school. Are they trying to crush me?

On the first visit, I meet my counselor and fill out some dumb questionnaires. The counselor seems to be pretty nice. I thought I would have to call her Dr. Whatever, but she said, "No, just call me by my first name, Kim, Mrs. Kim is fine."

The first session comes and goes without much being said, but the following week, boy, do I give Mrs. Kim an earful. I gripe about how it's not fair that my parents control my life, how they are making me come here by holding my car hostage. They are so unfair. Why can't they just leave me be? My grades are good, I'm popular, I don't get in trouble at school. What is their problem?

After all my complaining about my parents, she says something like, "So why do you think it is so important to them that you see me?"

"Because they want to rule my life," I explain.

"Is this the first time they have ever made you see a counselor?" she asks. "Are they really just that controlling, or is there a certain concern for you that is driving this? Like what particular behavior of yours are they concerned about? You say you are doing well in school, that's great. You are well-liked, that's good. Friends are important, and you don't get in trouble. Sounds like you are the perfect child to me. What do you think their issue is?"

"I don't know," I complain. "They're just dumb," I continue as my voice lowers and fades as I say that part.

"Well, we can explore that if you like, or we could just sit. Just sit and be present. Talk or not, whatever you like," she says.

So, we sit in silence for the rest of the hour. Time's up, and I leave. That may be a job I want! Get paid to just sit, say hi, and ask a few questions. Mrs. Kim knows where it's at. She worked hard to get where she is now, has her degree, and collects that money. My mom makes me go again, week after week. Sometimes, Mrs. Kim and I have small talk, and sometimes, we just sit there. Maybe I will become a counselor one day. Seems like easy money.

After a month of this and sitting in silence, I eventually get bored. I have to stay for an hour. It's a long time to just sit there in this little room with a person I don't really know, so I decide to study her office. You can learn a lot about a person by their belongings. Undergraduate diploma from Tulane University, that's in New Orleans, where Hurricane Katrina hit. How appropriate, Katrina started this disastrous life for me, ruining my plans and stealing my man. Counseling certification from Penn State. Looks like she likes to travel. There are things on her shelf from other countries: African-looking masks, Hindu artifacts, a huge beer mug from Germany, and lots of other neat-looking stuff.

Then again, there is only so much to look at. The ceiling tiles have caught my eye. They are white with little holes in them. There are 400 little holes in each tile and 80 tiles. It would be exactly 32,000 holes, but some tiles are cut, so they are not quite that many.

This is how my sessions have gone for quite some time. I study every inch of her office while she sits patiently. She asks a few questions that I give brief answers to.

"You should consider redecorating your office. Maybe change up the furniture." I realize I have nothing left in her office to memorize. I know every inch of it.

She looks at me.

"I mean, I like it like it is," I pause. "It's just a suggestion."

"It's fine," she says. "So apparently, you have memorized everything in my office and want something else to look at. Maybe now, since you have finished evaluating my office, you will be willing to start looking at yourself, a little self-evaluation?"

"Wow," I think to myself. "SNAP!"

We sit in silence for the rest of the hour. She has challenged me. She knew what I was thinking already. Maybe I will have to set her straight. She can't know what I am thinking, after all, she is a grown-up. They can't understand.

A week passes, and I arrive at my session ready to set the record straight. She cannot know what it is like to be me, she doesn't know. I sit down, and to my surprise, I do not say a word. My know-it-all attitude starts to slowly fade away. There is a kind of weird silence between us, then, I begin to fill it with words.

"It's like I have to be perfect because everyone tells me how lucky I am and how awesome I am, but I don't feel that way. Not really. I mean," I start spewing.

"I know I am smart and pretty, but so what? When I am alone, this darkness fills my head. I was just born this way. My mom is beautiful and intelligent, and my dad could be on the cover of GQ. So, I'm smart and pretty, so what?"

I can't believe that I am actually saying this out loud. I stop talking.

"So, how do you feel about that?"

"What do you mean? I just told you."

"Well, you said lots of things. But in a word or two, how do you feel about all that stuff? In a word or two, what are you feeling?"

"Well, what I really feel is pressure. Pressure to stay on top, but why, where does it get me, what does it matter? I am okay when I am

Surviving Sixteen

around others. I can put on a show when they are watching. But once I am alone, I wonder where my life is headed and what if this is the best it gets?" I spew my thoughts out without thinking.

"What are some things you do enjoy?" she asks.

"There are plenty of things I enjoy, but it doesn't matter. I am not happy!"

Silence fills the room. The African mask seems to laugh at me, mock me.

"What does that mean to you?" my counselor urges me to continue, "To be happy?"

I tell her about Jacob and Katrina and how they had a banner saying "Are you happy?" I do not want to go to New Orleans to help rebuild. That will not make me happy. How can that make me happy?

"I want you to think about this a little and maybe jot some ideas down. Keep a journal, if you will. It's time to go," she says. "We will pick this up next week."

Are you kidding me? I finally start spewing my guts out, and it's time to go. Argh! I am ready to get home and go to sleep.

Of course, that can't happen because we must have the Baxter family dinner. I sit and eat and tune out all of the noise. The fog has filled my head, and I feel like I am drowning in it.

"Nadia, it's your day to clean up," Mom announces.

## Surviving Sixteen

I get up and start the dishes. Dom jumps up and announces that he's going to help. What's the deal with this little guy? He jumps up, does the floss, and starts helping me. His actions clear some of the fog and we clean the kitchen together.

"Thanks, Dweeb." I envy him.

Things go on as usual, home, school, ball, family dinner, then sleep, my favorite part of the day. I am still forced to go to counseling once a week, but I don't hate it anymore.

My counselor asks a few questions to get me thinking, "Why such pressure to never fail? What would happen if you did fail? Wouldn't the world keep spinning?"

She also questions my being, who I am. "Whoever said that you have to always look perfect or put on a facade? So, what if someone knows you're having a bad day? Why always put on a show for everyone," Mrs. Kim questions me pausing after each question, prodding for a response.

"I can't think like that. I have to stay on top. Have to be...I don't know," I pause for a long while. "It's just so exhausting," I confess. "Sometimes, I just want to go to sleep and fade away."

Mrs. Kim sits up and makes a note. Oh no, I should not have said that!

I see that look of concern in her. "It's fine," I assure my counselor. I have no plan to hurt myself. These are just some of the thoughts in my head. I mean, think about it, things may get better, but if I go to sleep and never wake up, they definitely can't get worse."

This rant has my counselor a bit concerned, but I assure her it's just my way of trying to make sense of everything.

"Have you ever considered suicide or self-harm?" she asks very directly.

"No," I said and chuckled, trying to lighten the air and get myself out of trouble. "I would never end my life. But," I pause, "maybe I can sleep through it until it's time for me to go."

I realize that I am looking down. I sit up and try to justify my thoughts, "After all, isn't that our ultimate goal? To make it to heaven, if God's so great, and heaven is where we all want to go, that's where I want to be. Why can't I go there now? You know, it's just my logical side talking. I'm very cerebral."

I could tell Mrs. Kim isn't buying it, but it's true. I don't want to kill myself. I just don't really have a desire to live anymore.

I quickly change the subject, "Ms. Kim, you should have seen me at my last basketball game. It was great! The game came down to the wire, and I stepped up. I made the best steal of my life and an assist to Paulette to end the game. We won by one point! After the game, everyone was congratulating us. It was great."

I sat in silence for a few minutes, thinking. I then continued describing the events to Ms. Kim.

"Mom, Dad, and Dominic were there too. Dom came running up to me after the game," I shared excitedly. "I thought he was going to come congratulate me too, but no," my tone slows, and my voice lowers. "He just wanted to know if I felt better. Apparently, I'm not always so good at hiding my depression."

"You don't look sick anymore, so now, can we hang out? Can I ride home with you and sing and play Punch Buggy?" he asked me.

"What a Dweeb!" I grin as I think of him. "Made me smile though. He always makes me smile," I ramble on to Ms. Kim.

"I would like for you to journal about this," Ms. Kim says.

"About what, my game?"

"No. Dominic. I want you to see the world from his eyes. What do you think he sees, and what do you think he feels day to day and why?"

I look at Mrs. Kim with wonder.

"Why do you think he is the way he is?" she continues. "I notice you smile every time you talk about him. Let's look into this more."

So weird, I think. Why would I want to journal about Dominic? I mean, he is just a kid. What does he know? What worries does he have?

That night, I try it. I write in my journal.

Dominic, I don't know. He's a weird little kid. He always wants to play. He doesn't worry about what other people think. Why would he? He's just 8 years old. He doesn't know any better. Wait till he gets to high school. It can eat you alive, and he is always doing that silly dance. I guess it makes him feel good. It sure makes everyone around him laugh. He is always volunteering to help, too. What's wrong with that kid?

I doze off and wake up around midnight. I lock my journal away, and go to the bathroom, wash my face, and brush my teeth. On my way back to my room, I peek into Dom's room. He really is a good kid. Don't know what I'd do without him. I smile, head back to my room, and get a good night's sleep.

# Chapter 4
# Homecoming

I wake up bright and early the next day and head off to school. There is a pep in my step. I walk into the kitchen and see Dominic.

"I fixed your spot," he says. "I put out a bowl and your spoon, and here are three different cereals for you to choose from. Oh, wait! Let me get the milk. I kept it in the refrigerator so it would stay cold."

"What's up with you? Why are you always so nice to me?"

"It makes me happy to see you smile," he says.

I can't help but smile, and he giggles.

"Lucky Charms," I say. "I think today may be my lucky day. Lucky Charms for breakfast with my lucky charm brother. Today will be a good day."

We have breakfast together and are then off to school, singing the whole way and playing Punch Buggy. You wouldn't think there are that many VW Beetles out there, but we always see at least one or two.

When I arrive at school, I see my friends waiting for me. I walk up to them.

## Surviving Sixteen

"Let's SNAP to it, today is the day they announce Homecoming King and Queen."

"Oh yeah," Suzy says. "You are a shoo-in."

"Do you think Jacob will be the King?" Paulette asks.

"I don't know," I reply, "and I don't really care. I kind of hope not, but you know he will probably be named King. He's the favorite. Joey may have a chance. He's pretty cute. I wouldn't mind having him as my King."

Annie agrees, "He can be my King."

She has had a crush on Joey for quite some time now.

We walk into the school building, and everyone tells us hi. I am still on top. The Jacob thing is over, and I am over him. He is dating Katrina and they really have become the perfect couple. They are always together and always recruiting for that summer program. I just don't get it. How is volunteering and giving up your summer in some torn-up city a good idea? How is being in that depressing environment going to help anyone feel better? I will feel better chilling in my room, scrolling on my phone, and maybe going out for a manicure or pedicure now and then. Maybe I will even get a job at that cute little boutique. I would be able to get the employee discount and make a little money to treat myself to whatever.

The bell rings, and first hour begins the morning business with Spanish class. My favorite phrase is "Yo no se, which is I don't know." The boy's favorite thing to say is, "Puedo ir el Juan, por favor? Can I go to the John, please?" so immature.

Second hour comes and goes without incident, then third hour arrives. Miss Schwimmer, my science teacher, is teaching us about the circulatory system when suddenly her circulatory system stops working properly! At first, she just seemed to be a bit winded. Then, suddenly stops talking and collapses to the ground.

"Call the office," I scream out.

Someone pulls the switch, and the office responds, "Can I help you?"

"We need…Miss Schwimmer…she fell…she passed out…we need help," everyone is talking over one another.

Mr. Vander comes in from the room next door upon hearing the commotion. He calls 911. It seems like an eternity before anyone arrives. Mr. Vander begins CPR on Miss Schwimmer. I can hardly believe what I am seeing.

"Is she gonna die?" someone cries out.

"Shut up!" another person yells.

"Let's say a prayer for her," Katrina suggests and begins. "Our Father, who art in Heaven, hallowed be thy name."

Some of the students join in, but others just watch.

Mr. Vander ignores us all and continues doing CPR. We can now hear sirens in the distance. They are getting closer.

A fire engine arrives first, then, an ambulance and police car pull up around the same time.

"There's not a fire," some idiot calls out.

"Shut up," someone else says.

The firemen rush in and take over for Mr. Vander. They put some monitors on her, and we hear them say there is no pulse. They shock her two times as they continue pushing on her chest. She opens her eyes.

"Whoa," I think. "She was gone, and now she's back. Just like that, in an instant."

The class begins cheering and clapping softly. Everyone seems relieved but scared to make too much noise. After all, Miss Schwimmer does not like a noisy classroom.

The paramedics arrive with the stretcher and proceed to tend to and monitor Miss Schwimmer's stats. When they feel she is stable enough, they load her onto the stretcher and take her out to the ambulance.

The bell rings, and it's time to change classes.

"Let's go," Mr. Vander says. "Pack up and move along."

And that's it. Just like that, we watch someone be brought back from the dead, and all they say is to pack up and move along. What the hell?

I get to my next class and just sit there. Everyone is talking about what happened. People are saying she died on the way to the hospital. No one really knows what's happened. Rumors run rampant: she's fine, she died, she had a heart attack, she OD'ed.

I go through the rest of the day in kind of a daze. If she dies, what happens? Sure, I'm sure her family will be sad if she even has family. She has never been married and doesn't have children. We are her children, she would say. I guess they'll hire a new teacher. There is already a sub in her class now. Would we really miss her? I mean, no one really likes her anyway. She is so mean to everyone and she seems to truly hate us. I don't even know why she is a teacher. All she ever does is complain and tell us how we don't care about anything and won't amount to much if we stay on the path we are on. Maybe the world is a better place without her.

No, no, no, stop thinking like that. What is wrong with me? It's terrible what happened. A couple of students even checked out they were so upset. Damn, I must be a cold-hearted bitch.

But it's true, I can't stop my thoughts. The world just moves on. They just made an announcement that we will still be having our pep rally this afternoon. The world keeps turning even with one less person in it.

"Stop it, Nadia," I tell myself. "Miss Schwimmer's probably fine. Why are you so quick to write her off?"

The bell rings, and lunchtime arrives. The cafeteria is filled with people talking about today's events, with the ambulance, police cars and fire truck showing up.

"I wouldn't mind having one of those firemen named as the King of Homecoming," I say

"I know girl. Did you see that guy? He was so fine." Suzy agrees.

"Which one?" Paulette chimes in, "They were all so cute."

"Jon Wilma and Angel Morales," says Annie.

"What?"

"Jon and Angel, that's their names," Annie says. "I saw their name tag."

"You mean, while Miss Schwimmer was lying on the floor dying, you were checking them out, memorizing their names and everything?" I say.

"And you guys weren't?" she laughed. You started it. Saying you want him for your King."

"Well, SNAP" we all say at once as we snap our fingers together.

"Come on, let's go to the pep rally. It's time."

We get up and head to the gym. The cheerleaders and pep squad are already there dancing around, cheering, and welcoming everyone. I head to the locker room to get changed into my uniform. They always introduce both the girls' and boys' sports teams. When everyone arrives, our principal takes the mic.

"Settle down, everyone. Settle down. I have an important announcement to make before we begin. Most of you are aware of the incident we had today involving Miss Schwimmer. I am pleased to announce that we received a call from the hospital, and she is doing fine. She did have a heart attack, but thanks to the quick thinking on Mr. Vander's part and the quick response from 911, she is going to be fine."

Some teachers begin clapping, and students join in.

"She will stay in the hospital for a few days but is stable and sent a message for you to make sure you complete your homework tonight."

Lots of sighs follow this comment. I think he was joking, but I'm not really sure. She is the type that would send such a message.

Anyway, no time to think of this now. It's pep rally time. Teams are announced. The captains of both teams are announced first. That would be me and Paulette for the girl's team and Jacob and Joey for the boys. The cheerleaders do a couple of routines then the dance team performs. Some freshman boy runs out and joins in with the dance team.

"Wooo hoooo…" someone calls out.

"Get it, boy," another says.

He has the moves down pretty well. Everyone is laughing, but the principal motions to a teacher to get him out. She grabs him, and everyone boos. You never know what will happen at these pep rallies. One year, the seniors "pantsed" the freshman on the team. They were all standing there, in front of the whole school, in their underwear. It was epic. An epic punishment followed, and nothing quite as exciting has happened since then.

Finally, now is the time I have been waiting for. The principal takes the mic and says it's time to announce the Homecoming Court. First, he calls out every boy's and girl's name that made it onto the court in alphabetical order. No surprises there. We all kind of knew who would make it, even Katrina made the court. That's what happens when you date the most popular guy at school.

Now, it's time for the King and Queen to be announced. I know it would be Jacob and me if only we were a couple. No, maybe it will be Joey. That would be awesome. Not sure how much of a chance he has, but if anyone can beat Jacob it is him. In fact, Jacob may not be King. He may have sealed his fate when he decided to go steady with Katrina instead of me.

The principal speaks again, "And the King and Queen of our Homecoming Court this year is, drum roll please." He opens the envelope and reads the names, "Jacob Domiano and Katrina Boudreaux."

I lean forward to stand up when my ears hear that wretched, horrid name, Katrina Boudreaux. I lean forward and start to collapse my head into my hands when I realize that everyone is probably staring at me. I stand up and begin to clap.

"Yes!" I said. "I voted for you. You deserve it. You have been through so much. Congrats. How perfect!" I exclaimed.

I could see the look on my friend's faces. They knew me well, and they knew I was saving face. They went along with me.

"Yeah, that was a good idea to vote for her, Nadia. So thoughtful."

They go through the formalities, and my friends turn to look at me.

I hustle out of there. I couldn't stay any longer. The air began to get so thick around me that I could not breathe. The fog was smothering, the noise deafening. I rushed out to my car and drove home. I locked myself in my room and cried. I received lots of texts from my friends checking on me, but it just made it worse. How humiliating!!!

I finally fall asleep and don't wake up until the next morning. My mom had heard the news and decided not to bother me. Mrs. Kim had suggested she give me a little space.

At breakfast the next morning, my mom said she checked on me last night but didn't want to wake me up. Thought I could use the rest.

"By the way," she added. "I scheduled you an extra session with Mrs. Kim."

"Great," I thought to myself, "even my mom thinks I'm a loser."

I get up and leave for school. I don't even wait for Dominic. I'm sure I'll pay for that later, but I don't even care. My perfect mother can bring him. He's her son anyway. I am not up for his happy-go-lucky self.

I pull up to school and see Suzy, Annie, and Paulette hanging out in the parking lot. I can imagine what they are saying. I know what I would be saying if I were in their shoes. I park and grab my backpack, ready to get out and face my future, but quickly change my mind. I throw my backpack down, throw my car into reverse, and pull away. I honk twice as if to say, "See ya," and drive away.

I spend the rest of the school day at the riverfront. I write in my journal and think of Miss Schwimmer and Mrs. Kim. I am sure she will bring up the last session's comment I made about the end of life. I will be careful of what I say today. But really, what's the point? I begin writing in my journal to help organize my thoughts.

What is the point? Look at Miss Schwimmer, she has spent her whole career as a teacher and is terrible at it. She is a mean and miserable individual. No one would even miss her if she had died. They replaced her within 20 minutes. Look at me. Jacob had replaced me, and everyone bought into it. They all replaced me. I was supposed to be the Queen! I deserve it. I am tired of always trying to be perfect, nothing really helps anyway. You say things will get better, but I don't see it. They have just gotten worse. And so, what if it gets better and if I'm not around, I'll never miss it. If I could just go to sleep and never wake up again, I would be happy. That's what will make me happy. The world will go on without me. My family will be happier.

My mom and dad wouldn't have to spend their money on me going to therapy, it's not helping anyway. Dominic, that little Dweeb, he'll be happy no matter what happens. I just try to bring him down. I'm so jealous of his attitude. I will never be that way. It's not fair. I don't want to be here. I just want to be done.

I continue writing.

Don't worry. I would never kill myself. After all, you, Mrs. Kim, have ingrained some scary thoughts into my head. Out of the different philosophies on the afterlife, heaven is the one I like the most, or just being nothing. That would be fine, too.

But no, what about hell? Some people believe that suicide is automatic damnation, others believe in reincarnation. Who the hell would want to do this again and have to start all over? No, don't worry, too many bad options. With my luck, I'd end up worse off than I am. The way things are going, that's what would happen to me.

I look at my watch and realize it is time to go. My appointment will be starting soon, and it's across town. I tuck away my journal, walk to my car, and begin driving. I probably shouldn't be driving. I've been on an emotional roller coaster all day. I've been crying, and my eyes are swollen. I think about skipping, but I already have the appointment and I really need to talk. I have written down these thoughts, and now I must share them. But, I don't know if I can. I say I won't hurt myself, but I don't know how long I can go on feeling this way. I'm tired, just tired. I don't really want to exist. Things are just too hard.

I begin to drive. It's hard to focus on my driving. My eyes are swollen, and my mind is racing. The fog is dense and darker than usual. I come across the infamous stop sign that I hate, another damn dump truck coming. Almost bit the big one last time.

My mind is racing. My thoughts are too fast. Maybe if it's an accident, no one will ever know. God will understand. He won't send me to hell. I'm already in hell on earth. I see the dump truck barreling down the road. I know I need to stop. I begin slowing down, preparing to stop, but my mind is racing too fast. "What if you didn't stop? There would be no more, no more anything." I take my foot off the brake and accelerate. My car is now racing as fast as my thoughts. No time to think of consequences. We meet at the intersection.

# Chapter 5
# Reality

It is the loudest noise I've ever heard. Metal bending, crunching, screeching. If metal could scream, this is what it would sound like. It is deafening, and I black out.

Bright light slices through the blinks of my eyes, then, they blur. The ringing in my ears, I can't hear anything but the ringing. I try to understand what is going on. Where am I? What is happening? The stop sign, the dump truck. I didn't. I couldn't have. The ringing fades, and it all goes dark again.

I try to open my eyes, but it's difficult. I rub them and peel them open. Everything is upside down. Again, I try to make sense of things but cannot. Things sound way too far off. Why am I wet? Water? No, too thick and warm. But I feel cold, so cold now. Oh my God, what did I do? Things go dark again.

"Hello? Miss? Can you open your eyes? Open your eyes. Miss?"

"I'm sorry," I whispered when the realization of what I did slowly sinks in. "Please, tell my family I'm sorry. I never thought I would..." My voice fades away, and I sleep.

"Stay awake," he urges. "He rubs his knuckles across my breastplate, and it jolts me awake."

"That hurts! What are you doing? Why are you pushing on me? Stop it? Leave me alone," I think. Not realizing that he is trying to stop the bleeding and save my life.

I open my eyes wide, and they finally adjust. I see the man's name tag, Angel Morales, oh my gosh.

"Angel, my King. I'm ready. I'm just so tired. I didn't mean to do it, but I did. I am ready."

Angel calls out for a neck brace and saline, "She has lost lots of blood."

"Just please, please tell my family I'm sorry," I continue mumbling.

Angel continues talking, "Stay with us. Come on. What's your name?" He tries to keep me alert.

I close my eyes again. What did I do? What will people think of me? My thoughts race, then fade, then race again.

First responders are feverishly trying to save me, but my door won't open, and my legs are stuck and crushed under the dashboard.

"You have to stay with us," Angel says. "Open your eyes. Come on, you can do it. You aren't finished here. You have so much to do and so much to learn."

"No," I reply. "I'm done. I am tired and just want to sleep now. That will make me happy. Tell my family that I am sorry, but now I'm finally going to be happy. I am just so tired."

"What? What makes you happy?" Angel asks. "What do you like? What makes you smile? Come on. Hold on," Angel continues trying to reach me.

"Dom," I call out. Dominic and his playful, loving, and generous spirit I think to myself. Dominic, that's what makes me happy, I think as I smile and cry a single tear.

Angel watches the tear roll down my face, washing away a streak of the blood. "Dom," I say one last time and smile as I take my last breath, my big, brown, lifeless eyes wide open.

Angel and his colleagues work to extract Nadia.

"We have to save her. She did this on purpose. We can't let her die," Angel says aloud to no one in particular.

The first responders stabilize her neck and continue to put pressure on her wounds to slow the bleeding. They still cannot get her out of the car. The car is mangled beyond recognition. The jaws of life are brought out, but it's too late. Nadia is gone. Her bleeding has stopped because her heart has stopped. There is nothing to pump the blood anymore. No movement, nothing, nothing to stimulate her nerves, nothing to pump thoughts into her head anymore. Nothing there, just the physical body left in the vehicle.

The urgency that the men had worked has slowed. The drive that was rushing their work had disappeared along with this young lady's life. They finish their job, extract the body, and complete their job with an emptiness that they are all too familiar with. This one was tough. She was so beautiful and young, a whole life and world out there left for her to explore, cut short.

"This was intentional," Angel said. "Her parents will be devastated. Their life will be changed forever. How could she do this? She called out my name and confessed to me. She thought I was her King." Angel knelt on one knee, bowed his head, and said a prayer for the young lady.

As he gets up, he hears an officer saying he found her backpack and school ID. He will do the notification in person. The young fireman, Angel Morales, asks to join him.

"She spoke to me. I would like to go with you for the death notice. She obviously loved her family. I want them to know she was thinking of them. They are what mattered to her. And Dom, not sure who that is, but she kept calling out his name. And she smiled. That was the last thing she did. She said his name and smiled."

The officer agrees to allow Angel to accompany him. This is going to be a tough notification, and having Angel there may help. Upon the arrival of the Baxter home, the officer rings the bell. Mr. and Mrs. Baxter answered the door, curious to see who was ringing the bell at this time of day.

The Baxters's hearts sink as they see the police officer and young fireman. They know something terrible has happened.

The officer notifies them of the accident. They are also informed that it is being investigated as a possible suicide. They are told of the circumstances, that Nadia had slowed to a near stop then accelerated again, right into the path of the dump truck.

"There will be an official investigation, but it does not look good," the officer explains.

Angel Morales shares his message, telling them that Nadia insisted he tell them she was sorry, so sorry for what she had done and that she said she loved them.

Mr. and Mrs. Baxter take no solace in knowing this. The pain that they feel, the sickening feeling that pulls them to the ground, overcomes them both. Mrs. Baxter falls to her knees, and Mr. Baxter kneels over her. It is not certain if he is comforting her or using her strength to hold himself up.

"Noooooo," Mrs. Baxter cries out. The god awful feeling she has is indescribable.

Time seems to stand still, still and empty, unreal.

Mrs. Baxter gags from the tears and pain. Vomit spews out of the loss she feels. The dry heave comes next. She cannot control the violent reflex. Heave out the pain. Heave out the words she just heard. Heave out everything that hurts, the guilt and doubts about what they could have done better.

'No," she thinks to herself. "This was an accident. She did not do this on purpose. She could not have."

"Mom?" a sweet, concerned little voice calls out. Dominic is slowly easing his way down the stairs, scared to see what's wrong. "Mom? Dad?"

Mr. Baxter reaches out and grabs Dominic. "Oh, Dominic," he exclaims. Mr. Baxter does not want to let Dominic go but sends him to his room. "It's ok," he tries to assure him. "Go to your room. We will be there in a minute. Go. Let us finish talking to the officers."

"I'll go, but you have to let go of me!" Dominic pulls away from his dad and runs upstairs, worried and confused.

Angel, hearing the name Dominic, shares that Nadia had called out for Dom.

"Dom, she called out his name and smiled. She kept saying his name. He brought a smile to her face. I just thought you should know."

The officers left, and Mr. and Mrs. Baxter were left with not only the task of living without their beautiful daughter but must somehow, break the news to Dominic that he will never see his sister again. He is so young. He adores Nadia. How will they survive this? How would they go on without their baby?

Every second, minute, and hour that passes is full of darkness and dread and amplified by emptiness. So much is missing. How could this have happened?

No, they thought. This is not happening. But the pit in their stomach says it is. It had to be an accident and that's what they tell Dominic. It was a terrible accident.

Neither of them could understand Nadia taking her life. She had everything anyone could ever want. What more could they have done? What did they do wrong? They could not understand on one hand, but on the other, they seemed to have the same feeling of hopelessness and desperation. The thought of living without her seemed too much of a burden to bear.

No. Breaking down and giving up is not an option. They have to keep going. Dominic needs them now more than ever. He adored his sister. The Baxters protect Dominic from the reality of the situation the best they can.

"It was a terrible accident," they tell him. "Your sister loved you so, and she will always be with us in our memories. We will never forget her."

The Baxters put on a brave face and repeat their clichés to self-motivate.

"Make the most of the day. Take the bull by the horns. Use your time wisely." This is what they had taught Nadia, and it is what would help them move forward.

The funeral was sad yet beautiful at the same time. There was a slideshow of pictures showing Nadia at different ages and stages in her life. She had done so much in the short 16 years she spent on this earth. The support and love the Baxters felt from all of the guests was undeniable. It seems as if every student from her high school has shown up. The administration, teachers, and Coach Macy were there, too. It made the Baxters proud of their little girl to see how much the people around her cared.

Nadia's best friends, dubbed SNAP, had sat in the front row the entire service. They spoke with Dominic and assured him that Nadia had always enjoyed her time with him. They went on and on, telling him all sorts of stuff and stories. Some were stories that had actually happened, like the dancing in the frozen yogurt store, and some were just things they had just made up. Stuff to make him feel better. They knew it was all the stuff Nadia would have said if she were actually there.

"She loved playing Punch Buggy and tag," Suzy says.

"She told us that you were the nicest kid she knew," Annie chimes in. "She never understood how, no matter what she did to you, or how rotten she treated you, you always seemed to be there for her."

"Yep, you helped her with the dishes and made her laugh when she was sad. She said you were her special little pain in the butt that she loved," adds Paulette.

The girls would be strong and talk so happily when Dominic was sitting with them, then would boo-hoo and cry when he would run off. He came and went, and so did their emotions, just like a roller coaster.

"We are SAP," says Suzy.

"What?" asks Annie.

"SAP?" questions Paulette. "What are you talking about?"

"We went from SNAP to SAP. We are just sad SAP. We lost our N," Suzy cries.

"I hope she's happy. I hope she's happy now. Just look at what she did. Why did she do it? What the hell?"

The accident had officially been ruled a suicide. The brakes on the car were inspected. There was nothing wrong with them. The report from the driver of the dump truck, Nadia's journal, and her own words to Angel had brought the coroner to label the death a suicide.

Disbelief filled the air, and the word suicide itself was not dared spoken at the funeral. It was just a terrible accident and a huge loss, one that no one seems to understand.

# Chapter 6
# Dominic

The Baxter's had great intentions. They planned to live by all of the cliches they had preached, but the despair was overwhelming. The sadness brought on some depression of their own. Mr. and Mrs. Baxter each dealt with things their own way and went through their own stages of grief. Mr. Baxter became angrier and angrier, and Mrs. Baxter carried more sadness and guilt.

Dominic was told that Nadia's death was an accident, but heard the rumors about suicide. Dominic struggled, he did not know what to think or believe. He looked to his parents for support, but they were so caught up in their own anger, sadness, and guilt that they could not give him what he needed. Dominic tried being a good son. He wanted to fix things. He wanted to make his mom and dad laugh and smile, but they didn't seem to notice, or they would tell him, "Not now, Dominic, go play."

Dominic became withdrawn and lonely. He missed his sister so much, and now it seemed as if he lost his parents too. He reverted back to wetting the bed. He always tried to change and wash his pajamas and sheets on his own. He didn't want to be a burden, but one of his parents would always catch him.

"I'm sorry. I didn't mean to," he would cry.

And all his parents would say was that it was alright and "Let's get cleaned up."

He hated that he was a baby and felt like a burden.

One day at school, the assignment was to draw a family picture. Dominic drew himself in front of a huge house. He drew his mom lying down in a room and his dad sitting at a desk in his office. He had drawn something else, but had drawn and erased it so many times the teacher was not able to make out what it was. He had actually erased a hole in the paper.

"What was this going to be?" the teacher questions him.

"It's a hole," Dominic replies.

"I see it is a hole, but what was it before you erased it?" she asks ever so kindly.

Dominic looks up at her and says, "It was my sister, Nadia, but she's not here anymore. It's just a hole."

The teacher softly rubs Dominic's back and moves on so as not to cause a scene. She then quietly calls the school counselor, who immediately calls Dominic in.

"Hi, Dominic. I wanted to talk to you about this drawing. It's a great drawing. Can you tell me about it?"

"Well, that's me. I'm outside."

"Do you like it outside? I like the outdoors," she adds.

"I like outside. I like riding my bike and climbing trees."

"But you look a little sad. Why do you have a frown in the picture?" she gently pries.

"Lately, people always come over to talk to Mom and Dad and they tell me to go outside and play. Even if I don't want to."

"I see. Who are the other people in your drawing?"

"That's my mom lying in her bed. She sleeps a lot but my dad says she's okay, and that's my dad in his office. He likes to do his work where it is quiet," Dominic points to each as he describes them.

"What happened here?" the counselor asks as she points to the hole in the paper.

"Nothing," Dominic replies.

"It looks like you drew something there. What was it?"

"Well, it was my sister, but she's not here anymore. So, I kind of just erased her." Dominic stops talking and then adds, "I drew her because I think of her all the time, and my mom and dad say she is still part of our family, but I erased her because, well, because, you know why," Dominic mumbles the last part.

"Yes, I heard," the counselor confirms. "I wonder how you feel about that?"

Dominic slouches down in his chair and tries to hold back his tears.

"I wonder if the hole in your paper is like the hole you feel without your sister being there?"

Dominic cries and shouts at the same time. "I should erase my mom and dad too because it's like they are not here anymore either. It's not like it used to be."

There are a few moments of silence, and then Dominic breaks down even more.

He says the following so rapidly it is hard for the counselor to make out what he is saying while crying and yelling at the same time, "Why did she leave me? She was supposed to bring me to school that day. I could have kept her safe. She just left me! Why didn't she love me?" Dominic's tears flow freely and his nose begins running, too. It is heart-wrenching. "And my parents, they aren't the same either. I think they loved her more." Dominic can barely get his words out, "Can we try again? I'll do better. I can be a better brother."

"Oh, sweet boy," the counselor says and hugs Dominic, trying to console him.

The two of them talk for a while, and Dominic calms down a bit. The counselor gets him to talk about some of the good memories he has of Nadia. She also asks him to draw a picture of the two of them together, a happy time.

Dominic takes his time and draws the best he can.

"This is us doing the floss," he laughs as he shares his picture. "I know she loves that dance. She said she thought it was dumb, but I know she liked it. You see her smile?"

Dominic smiles and feels slightly relieved for the first time since losing Nadia.

The counselor sends Dominic back to class and reaches out to the Baxters. She knows that Nadia's death was a suicide. Dominic was correct, Nadia did choose to leave and that is hard for everyone to accept.

The counselor calls the Baxters to explain, "Many families struggle when they lose a child. Siblings are sometimes considered the forgotten mourners, not that you would ever forget about Dominic. It is just that the death is so much, and everyone needs their own time to heal."

"It has been quite overwhelming," the Baxters admit.

"It is often difficult for the parents to deal with the siblings' emotions because they are dealing with their own overwhelming emotions. It is quite natural. I would like to help. May I have your permission to work with Dominic?"

The Baxters meet with the counselor and agree to her assistance, but they insist she does not use the word suicide. They only want him to know that it was a terrible accident. She discusses the pros and cons of keeping him in the dark, but they insist.

"He is not to be told that she intentionally took her life. No one can prove that anyway. It was a terrible accident," Mrs. Baxter weeps.

"It is ultimately your decision, and I will respect your wishes."

Counseling begins, and Dominic learns to deal with his loss, the loss of his sister, and the family they once had. In fact, with time, the family slowly improves. Nothing will ever be the same, and the hole they feel will always be there, but somehow, their days improve, and they learn to live again. Family dinners and ice cream runs happen again, the bedwetting stops and they are able to get into a new family routine. Things have definitely improved, but the scars are always present and often open up.

As the years pass, Dominic still hears whispers about Nadia committing suicide, and his thoughts always race. He is older now and often wonders if it's true. He cannot comprehend her choosing to leave him and his parents. Of course, she didn't want to die. It was a terrible accident, he assures himself. It is what he had heard his mom say a million times.

"Why are people so dumb?" he would ask himself. "Why do they keep saying that about Nadia?"

Then, his thoughts would turn, "Maybe I am the dumb one."

There is always a little tapping on the back right side of his head. Tap, tap, tap…. It mocks him, dividing the word into the rhythm of a car blinker…Su..i…cide, tap, Su…i…cide. It taps into his brain. It is like the driver who forgets his blinker is on. Even if he doesn't know it is on, there it is, blinking for all the world to see. Blink, blink, blink, tap, tap, tap.

Once, Dominic asked his parents about Nadia's death being a suicide. They just hugged him and cried. He never asked again, and even though they hadn't spoken any words their silence was deafening. There it is. The blinker flashing for all the world to see.

I know people look at me and judge, Dominic thinks to himself. Do you know your blinkers on? Why can't you fix it? It makes him so angry and sad at the same time. He pushes the thoughts away and tries to ignore the tapping. The denial kind of helps him feel better but kind of makes him feel worse. What difference does it make, he wonders? It's still flashing for all to see.

Dominic hates being asked if he has any brothers or sisters.

"What do I say?" he talks to himself. "The answer is awkward no matter what. I can say I'm an only child. It's true, but not true. I can say that I had a sister, and she died. That then forces the person to tell me how sorry they are and ask what happened. I then tell them it was a terrible accident, and later they run off and talk to someone to find out the terrible accident was that Nadia did it on purpose! She pulled in front of that dump truck on purpose. She basically committed suicide. Do I just tell them she committed suicide? Oh, the look on their face if I said that!"

It is a constant struggle for Dominic, but he somehow continues moving forward. He decides to "Take the bull by the horns and make the best of things."

He manages, and before you know it, Dominic is the one waking up, showering, having breakfast, and going to high school. He has matured from a pretty good kid into a nice young man. It has been about 8 years since the death of his sister, and of course, it is not always easy, but he has ignored that tapping in his brain enough to get along pretty well. He gets good grades, has lots of friends, and is a savior for his parents. He still has a happy-go-lucky attitude in the way he approaches things, and it is refreshing. Don't get me wrong, he is still a typical teen and moody at times, but overall, he still has that loving, helping spirit.

Dominic's parents wonder how much he remembers his sister. What they wouldn't do to have her back again? She had so much talent and love to bring to the world. She had the world at her fingertips but didn't know how to reach out and grab it. The emptiness remains day to day. It never lets up.

The debilitating pain comes and goes and eases with time but is always present. The memories remain, always good thoughts to begin with, but then the reality that she will never be there to create new memories always spoils the thoughts. There will always be something missing. Nadia has taken so much away from her family, where she had so much to give.

## Surviving Sixteen

The night the Baxter's have been dreading for years has finally arrived. Dominic brings up a topic that they both knew was coming.

"I was wondering if one of you could bring me to take my driver's test on Saturday. I've finished my driver's ed program at school, and I think I'm ready. Aren't you tired of having to drive me around everywhere?"

The clinking of a fork hitting the plate rings out a high-pitched sound, and then silence fills the room.

"Well? Can you?" Dominic asks.

Mrs. Baxter gets up from the table, excuses herself, and hurries off to her room, leaving Dominic and his dad at the table.

"What's up with her?" Dominic asks.

"She would drive you around forever to help keep you safe. Let's talk as we do the dishes," his dad says.

"It's your turn," Dominic says.

"You know," Mr. Baxter replies, "you used to like helping. You saved your sister's hide many times when she was your age. Besides, didn't you say you wanted my help this weekend? Well, I want your help now. And... we need to talk."

"Oh boy," Dominic thought. "I'd rather clean up by myself, spare me the expense of a talk."

Mr. Baxter used this time to discuss the events of the past, and the struggles Nadia was having at the time of her death. The fact that she may have been distracted while driving and could have prevented the accident if her head was in the right place. It wasn't, and she did something very dumb and selfish.

"Your mom will never admit it, but Nadia's death was ruled a suicide. She pulled in front of that truck on purpose," Mr. Baxter is finally ready to say the words.

Dominic did not want to hear it. The tapping in the back right side of his brain is back. Tap, tap, tap...He had heard the rumors and pushed them away. What was his dad now telling him? Nadia would not choose to leave him. Tap, tap, tap. Reality was setting in and could no longer be denied.

Mr. Baxter went on to explain that driving is a huge responsibility with huge consequences. Driving must always be done with care, good intentions, and respect for life. The conversation went on like this the entire time they cleaned.

Dominic continues going through the motions of cleaning while feeling everything go numb and silent. Not really a true silence, there's a distant echo of his dad giving life lessons. How could she have done that to them? She had everything she could ever want. Dominic's anger grew, his face began to turn red and burn. Was it anger or sadness? Dominic couldn't tell.

This was not the first time he had heard about what Nadia had done, but it was the first time he let it sink in. He finished the dishes, turned, and stared at his dad, face burning, eyes welled up. His dad reached out to hug him and Dominic pushed him away. He began beating on his chest, crying out that horrible cry that he and his wife had cried so many times.

"Why? Why didn't you tell me?" Dominic cried out, which soon turned to, "Why? Why DID you tell me?"

A hundred more pounds on his dad's chest. The energy drained from his arms and then his body. Mr. Baxter grabbed Dominic and held him up as he sobbed.

Dominic went to bed that night with so much on his mind. His mom running out like that, the speech from his dad, the rumors and whispers that he heard years ago were true. Nadia had really left them. A new sense of emptiness filled Dominic's body. The thoughts he had haunted his dreams that night.

It had been years since Dominic had seen Nadia last, but in the dream, he could see her clear as day, as if she were standing right there, looking into his soul with those deep, dark brown eyes.

"The joke's on me," Nadia said to Dominic in his dream. "It's not any better."

She is standing there in her little skater skirt.

"I'm so sorry, Dom," she said as a single tear rolled down her face.

Dominic looks at her in disbelief.

Nadia continues talking, "You keep being you. Keep smiling and helping others. I will see you again soon," Nadia assures him.

Dominic closes his eyes and opens them again. They are not in his room anymore. Both he and Nadia are driving in a Volkswagen Beetle. "How do you like my punch buggy?" she asks.

"Why did you leave me?" Dominic asks. "That day, you were supposed to bring me to school. Why did you leave me? I could have helped you. Now look at what you've done!" he cries out in his little eight-year-old childlike voice.

Nadia slams on the brakes, and they are now in the kitchen washing dishes together.

"You are right, Dom. You always made things better. And I know you will always be there for me."

"I don't understand what happened. Why didn't you come to me? I could have helped you. I should have helped you," Dominic now says in his deepened sixteen-year-old voice.

"It's not your fault. It's no one's fault. I need to learn to stick it out and be there for you and others. I needed more time. I am so sorry I hurt you. Maybe one day I will learn."

Nadia fades away, and Dominic suddenly wakes up.

"Go away! I hate you!" he cries out.

Dominic sits up in his bed and cries until his anger subsides.

"I love you," he says aloud. "I miss you."

Heartache overcomes Dominic, and he cries himself back to sleep.

Dominic wakes the next morning with a lot on his mind. He has a vague memory of his dream. He is still angry, mad at Nadia and himself. A deeper sense of sadness overcomes him, an agony no one can know fills his being. The thought of getting his license made him physically ill. He stayed in his room that weekend and told his parents that he had some kind of stomach virus.

The weekend came and went, and no discussion of the driver's test was even brought up. In fact, weeks and months went by before the conversation of Dominic getting his license arose again. Dominic had too many feelings that he had to deal with. It took time, quite some time to absorb and adjust to his new reality.

Some depression set in, but he was able to push through it. His only wish was that Nadia could have done the same. It is hard to understand why she didn't or couldn't, but he is trying to forgive her.

# Chapter 7
# The Sassos

It is the summer before Dominic's senior year, and Mr. Baxter takes charge. He walks in from work one day and proclaims, "I think it's time, Dominic. We need to keep moving forward. Get up, take the bull by the horns. Let's go get that driver's license."

Yes! Dominic was ready. He had turned 17 and did not have his license yet. He had been thinking about it for a few weeks now but didn't know if he should bring it up again after what happened the first time. The response it elicited from both his mom and dad and the emotions it forced him to face were, well, just too much. He had gone through the stages of grief over his sister once when he was eight and then again at 16. It was slightly easier the second time because so many years had already passed, and he was used to it being just the three of them, he and his mom and dad, but it was also much harder because he knew what it meant.

She had chosen to leave. He was angry for quite some time, but he knew he had to move on. The anger faded, but fear took its place. It was an underlying fear that Dominic was not even truly aware of, a fear of losing anyone close to him.

"My driver's license? Yes! I'm ready. Let's do it. This is awesome!" Dominic declares.

Dominic passes his driving test easily. They call his mom to share the good news, "Want to meet us? We are going to get ice cream to celebrate!" Mr. Baxter says.

"I got my license!" Dominic screams into the phone.

A little touch of freedom is what Dominic is thinking to himself. Freedom to drive myself where I want to go, when I want to go and right now, I want ice cream.

"Sure, I'll come meet you. Where to?" Mom replies.

"You stay right there. We are coming to pick you up."

Dominic is a natural. He accelerates at a good pace and stops smoothly. He uses his mirrors and blinkers like a pro. Mr. and Mrs. Baxter are impressed. It was a nice night. The three of them reminisce about the good old days. Dominic shared his memories of Nadia driving him to school and how they always played Punch Buggy or sang loudly whenever she drove him. He told his parents that he knew he was young when she passed, but he remembers everything about her and has a sense that she is still around.

"Oh, Dom," Mrs. Baxter whispers as a tear runs down her face.

His mom had never called him by that name, only Nadia used to. This was another sign to Dominic that his sister was still with him. It made him feel so many different types of emotions to hear her say that name.

Senior year begins, and Dominic is so excited. He has most of his credits to graduate and looks forward to having a half day. He has been watching seniors leave early from high school for three years now. Now, it's his turn, and it's great! He leaves early, goes home, eats a snack, and plays video games until dinner. What more can a teenage boy want? His parents suggest he get a part-time job or a hobby, but why? This is the life, he thinks to himself, and he ignores their suggestions.

Dominic loves his schedule, driving himself to school, passing his classes with ease, playing video games, and then dinner. After dinner is the hardest part, motivating himself to study and shower. By then, it's bedtime, only to wake up and repeat the next day. Again, what more could a guy want?

After a few months of this, the days seem to feel longer. They tend to drag on. He wonders what it's all about. He begins sleeping in the afternoon. He thinks about his sister and how he misses her. He thinks about what she did and still wants to believe it was an accident. He is getting tired of the day-to-day, just like she was, but he could never imagine doing what she did, and his parents could not handle it. Just keep on moving, he tells himself. The air seems to lighten when he is moving.

Dominic's parents notice his lethargy and are aware of the warning signs of teen depression. They can see him fighting it, still performing well in school and participating in family dinners, but locking himself in his room. His lack of interest in doing things he used to love scares them. They take action.

"Dominic, we signed you up for a program. It's called Seniors Helping Seniors. Since you have so much free time on your hands and you have not taken it upon yourself to get a part-time job or find a new hobby, we found one for you," Mr. Baxter informs him.

Dominic was not happy about this, thinking he had his own issues to deal with.

"It will be a good experience for you," Mrs. Baxter adds.

Being a teenager can sometimes be all-consuming. Adults have lots of responsibilities and concerns, but teens have their own version of issues. Sure, they do not have the responsibilities of an adult, but they do not have the freedom of an adult either. They depend on their parents so much. It's like they are stuck between the freedom of being a carefree child and the freedom of being an adult, suffering and owning their own consequences.

"Parents just don't understand. How could they forget so quickly?" he wonders.

So, as things go, Mr. and Mrs. Baxter make Dominic join the program. He could choose not to, but after all, they control everything. It's their roof that he lives under, their money that he spends, the food he eats, and his car is really their car in their name. Dominic decides to do what they want, but he won't be happy about it.

Seniors Helping Seniors is a program that was designed for elderly seniors and high school seniors in Dominic's situation. High school seniors have their health and can help the elderly shop for groceries, clean houses, cut grass, or whatever needs to be done. The elderly seniors need assistance yet also have plenty to give. They have the experience and wisdom to help students grow emotionally. It is a win-win situation.

Dominic begrudgingly starts participating. He was assigned to Mr. and Mrs. Sasso. They were an elderly couple that had been married for 65 years. The husband used a walker and could barely get around. It hurt just to watch him walk. The wife was better but could not drive and depended on others to deliver groceries and medications to them.

Once a week, Dominic visited the Sasso's to check on them or make deliveries. It was the same thing every time, he would knock on the door, and Ms. Sasso would answer. Dominic would then enter with the groceries, set them on the kitchen table, then say hello to Mr. Sasso, who was always sitting in his chair watching an old-fashioned black and white tv show. After a month of "knocking and dropping," that's what Dominic called it, "the knock and drop," Dominic noticed that Mr. Sasso was not in his chair.

"Do you need anything else, Mrs. Sasso?" Dominic asked. "Is Mr. Sasso ok?"

"If you could wait just a minute to say hi to my husband that would be great. He just loves seeing you. He says you're such a nice young man."

"Sure," Dominic agreed and stood awkwardly waiting for Mr. Sasso.

"Let me fix you some tea," Mrs. Sasso insists.

"Sure," Dominic says as he awaits, thinking it would be a glass of iced tea.

Mrs. Sasso takes out a pot, fills it with water, and sets it on the stove.

"It will be just a minute," she says and walks into the back room to check on her husband.

Dominic takes in a deep breath and thinks he has probably made a mistake. Why did I say I could wait? Tea? Yes, iced tea. I think she is brewing tea. I didn't even know people still did that. "A cup of tea?" His thoughts have turned into an English accent now.

Mr. Sasso enters the room and says, "Hi there, young man. My wife tells me that you have a few minutes to spare and sit with an old man."

Not knowing how to reply, Dominic shuffles his feet and makes a gesture, finally saying, "Yes, I am going to have a cup of tea."

Dominic watches Mr. Sasso slowly shuffle across the room. The way he moves looks so painful, and it actually was very painful for Mr. Sasso, although Dominic acts as if it were just as painful to watch.

OMG, I couldn't handle it, Dominic thought as he watched Mr. Sasso struggle to get across the room. Why did I agree to tea? I just want to go home and chill.

Mr. Sasso finally arrives at his chair. It is one of those remote chairs that shifts upward to make it easier to get in and out. Mr. Sasso sits back and presses the button on the remote control. The chair begins to recline to a normal position, slow and steady, creaking a little as it lowers.

"'Sit," Mr. Sasso demands.

"Yes, sit," Mrs. Sasso says excitedly. "How do you like your tea?"

Cold, thought Dominic, but he politely replies, "However you make it is fine. I've never really had a cup of hot tea before."

"Oh, well, you are in for a treat," Mrs. Sasso replies.

Finally, settled into his chair, Mr. Sasso begins telling Dominic stories from his past. At first, all Dominic could do was think about and pity this old man. He could barely even get around, much less do any of the things he spoke of so fondly.

Mrs. Sasso delivers the tea to Dominic. He takes a sip, and the warmth travels down into his chest. It seems to relax him a bit. He sits back, a little more relaxed, and continues listening to stories. Dominic starts getting sucked in, imagining how things were and the Mr. Sasso of years past. He imagined him being young and strong. Before you knew it, two hours had passed.

"Oh, my goodness. Mr. and Mrs. Sasso, I hate to run, but I have to go. I have to complete a homework assignment to turn in before dinner time."

"Well, we sure thank you for your company," Mrs. Sasso says.

"Do you know how to play chess?" Mr. Sasso asked. "I love to play chess. So much strategy involved."

"No sir," Dominic replies, "but maybe you can teach me next time."

Dominic left the Sassos with a new feeling. It was a feeling of fullness. He had entered into a world he had never been before, hot tea and stories from way back when. It left an impression. The stories Mr. Sasso shared were so real. They came to life. Dominic went home with a pep in his step and a new appreciation of life and hot tea.

Before you know it, the days of "knock and drop" were over. Dominic began visiting the Sassos twice a week, once to bring groceries and once to visit and play chess. He enjoyed his time there. It seemed like a type of escape from his everyday humdrum life. Dominic was totally present when he was there. It was just the three of them in their own little world. No one or anything else existed for those couple of hours. Mrs. Sasso would serve a snack and a cup of tea, and Mr. Sasso would talk about the good and bad times.

Eventually, Dominic entrusted the Sassos with his stories. He even shared his fondest memories of his sister and shared the actualization of what she had done.

Dominic didn't really know why these visits helped him so, but from the outside looking in, you could see. The Sassos seemed to help Dominic place his thoughts into perspective. He used to feel helpless and sometimes worthless, wondering what life was all about. But finding the Sassos helped him realize some things. Life is not just about living for yourself. It's not only about doing the things you want to do.

Sometimes, it is about others and how they feel and what you can do for them. When he stopped thinking about himself and started thinking about others, it made him feel good. He had a purpose. Life had a purpose: to be there for one another. In fact, it reminded him of what his sister used to say about him…. "You are always making me smile and always helping me. What would I do without you?"

Nadia saying, "What would I do without you," flashed in Dominic's memory. At first, it made him happy and smile, but then came the anger. Why would she do such a thing?

"What would I do without you? What a crock!" he whispered to himself. "You left me!" he grumbled in a whisper as if she were standing right there.

Mr. Sasso could see Dominic's demeanor change and knew he was thinking about Nadia. "I am right here. Stop focusing on what you cannot control. Your sister is gone, but you're not, and neither am I," Mr. Sasso preached. "Make your life what you want it to be. Do something! Don't get too caught up in your sad or angry thoughts. Do something! If you cannot do anything to help yourself, then find something you can do to help others. It will come around. And right now, it is playing chess with me. Now, it's your move. Do!"

Dominic snapped out of it, he chuckled a little and moved his chess piece. The next move was Mr. Sasso's, and he did not hesitate to teach another lesson.

"Checkmate," he says. "You lost your focus, and look at what happened. Live in the present and do something. Stop sitting around and worrying about things you cannot control. Life is what you make it, not what you think about."

From that point on, Dominic had a new mantra. Do! That two-letter word became a powerful motivator for Dominic. Whenever he got stuck in his own thoughts, he would shake his head and remind himself of those two little letters, the first two letters of his name.

Dominic knew his time at home was short. He had received a scholarship and would be heading off to college soon. He used his last summer to do something a little special. He earned enough money to purchase a laptop for the Sassos and pay for a year's worth of internet. He spent lots of his time with them too, teaching them how to navigate the internet and, most importantly, how to get to the online chess game. Mrs. Sasso even taught Dominic how to brew his own tea.

"It can help you with your studies," she explained. "The coffee and pills you kids take nowadays to stay awake are not good for you. Trust me. This tea will change your life," she chuckled.

The Sassos already changed his life. They reminded him of what life was about. Dominic and the Sassos were another success story for the Seniors Helping Seniors program. They had enriched each other's lives in ways they couldn't foresee.

# Chapter 8
# Do

Dominic flourished with his new mantra. It helped him accomplish great things. It got him through college and into law school. No matter his age or location, he could imagine Mr. Sasso fussing, encouraging him. Life is about doing, he would say, doing for yourself and doing for others. Stop worrying so much and get off your keister and do! They would often quote Audrey Hepburn, "You know Audrey would say that as you grow older, you will discover that you have two hands, one is for helping yourself, the other for helping others. The earlier you learn that the better off you will be."

Dominic kept in touch with the Sassos while in college via telephone calls once a week and an online chess match with Mr. Sasso on the first Saturday of each month. It was hard for him not to see them or his parents regularly, but he knew he had to live in the present. He could not keep looking back and worrying about things he couldn't control, so he took what he could get.

Dominic had his ups and downs, just like every college student, but he did well for himself. He partied a little too hard every now and then and had a couple of girlfriends, none too serious. Said it was because he was too caught up in his studies, but the fear of losing another person so close to him was what really kept him single.

## Surviving Sixteen

Dominic attended all of the collegiate basketball games. It made him remember his sister in such a fond way. Made him feel close to her. It was something that she loved and was good at.

Dominic took the lessons he had heard throughout his life and decided Audrey was right, one hand was to care for himself and the other to help others. This was a driving force in his studies and decision to become a lawyer. He excelled in his classes, and now it was time to put his knowledge to the test. Passing the upcoming Bar Exam was Dominic's next big task.

One night, while prepping for the Bar, Dominic received a call from his mom and sent her straight to voicemail. He had to focus, he thought. Many people had to take the Bar a number of times, but he would not. He was determined to pass it the first time. So, when his mother rang a second time, he swiped it to voicemail once again. That call was followed by a text, "Dad and I are fine, but call ASAP."

Dominic calls his mom immediately, and she informs him that Mr. and Mrs. Sasso had passed away. There was an electrical fire at their home, and they were not able to get out. He was found in his bed, and she was sitting in a chair right there next to him. They believe they both died of smoke inhalation before actually burning. This knowledge had brought some, but little, relief to Dominic.

Dominic was devastated. He knew their limitations and was worried about how they would get along without him, but he had never even thought of such a tragedy. He knew Mrs. Sasso could have probably escaped the fire but refused to leave without Mr. Sasso. They adored one another. That's why they found her body in a chair next to him. God rest their beautiful souls.

Dominic felt this great loss and thought of his sister. The hole inside him seemed to grow larger. How hard it had to be for Mrs. Sasso to stay by his side the entire time until death overcame her. His own sister could not do that. She had chosen to leave him. He would never find a love like the Sassos had.

Dominic knew the importance of the exam coming up, and he had to prepare, but it was just too hard to focus, and his mind started wandering. He went to bed that night with a heavy heart. He tried to keep studying, but part of the mantra was to do for yourself also. He just needed time to grieve and rest.

After a few days of moping about, Dominic knew that he needed to get back to his studies but could not quite convince himself to get busy. He did the bare minimum to get by and moped a little longer than necessary. It's so easy to get into a slump. That night, Dominic had only been asleep for a short while before Mr. And Mrs. Sasso appeared to him in a dream. To Dominic, it did not feel like a dream, it felt so real. They were standing there right in his room.

"Get up," Mrs. Sasso said. "Go make yourself a cup of hot tea and stop your whining."

Mr. Sasso chimes in, "You have to keep going. Don't forget to DO! You can do so much. You helped me forget about my pain for a while. You fed us, and you nourished our hearts and souls. Get up, stop wallowing, and get out there. Do, Dominic," he said, "Do!"

Dominic did just that. He awakened with a new sense of purpose and determination. He popped out of bed and made himself a pot of tea. He had worked so hard to be where he was, and he was not giving in that easily.

The morning of the Bar Exam, Dominic was ready. He entered confidently and stayed focused, recalling the laws and codes of the criminal justice system at will. After the test, he went out to celebrate with a few friends, and the conversation turned to one of their futures. Dominic had given some thought about moving to D.C. and maybe eventually getting into politics where he could really make a difference, but the dream he had of the Sasso's reminded him of how much he missed his parents and his hometown.

"There is plenty of work wherever we go. I want to make a difference," Dominic states his true thoughts to his friends. "I may go back to my hometown. I really liked it there and want to spend more time with my parents while I can."

"That's sweet," Dominic's friend says, "but I'm going where the money is. I want to make a difference in my pocketbook!"

"I'll toast to that," another comments.

They clink their bottles and continue to laugh and drink, maybe a little too much that evening, but it is well deserved.

For the next ten weeks, Dominic anxiously awaited the results of his Bar Exam. He was confident on the day of the test, but the wait was causing his confidence to waiver. One thing had become clear during this time, he would move back home. In fact, he had already sent in his application to a number of firms. Finally, the envelope that Dominic had been waiting for arrived. He rips into it.

"Yes! I did it!" he cheers with relief.

"I did it, I did it, yes, yes, yes," he begins to sing, and before he realizes, he is doing the floss, his old, go-to dance move.

Dominic passed the bar on his first attempt, moved back to his hometown, and landed a job at an impressive law firm. He was the youngest lawyer there. He had gone through an accelerated program and succeeded with flying colors.

With Dominic's success came respect. He was a go-getter, and the partners at the firm loved his attitude and work ethic. Dominic also loved the work he was doing but continued having a nagging feeling that there was more. He and his colleagues had already donated lots of their time to some pro bono work. It was something they prided themselves on.

Dominic wanted to take it a step further. He had heard that the Seniors Helping Seniors program no longer existed, and since this was a major contributor to his success, he knew he had to do something. He wanted to offer something like it to other students out there. He prepares a plan and presents it to the partners.

"Lots of teens are lost. If they could get out and do something for others, it could change their lives. There are so many things that they need to see and experience. What better way than to see life through someone else's eyes? To see that they do matter to this world. They matter to each other, and the best way to learn this is to get up and 'DO…. Donate Oneself.'"

The senior partners thought this was a great idea and the law firm sponsored the non-profit organization, DO...Donate Oneself. The program will be a reminder to the public to reach out and get involved. Advertisements will advocate for individuals to share their abilities, help their neighbors and to get involved with other non-profit organizations.

Dominic really wanted to focus on high schools. The influence the Sassos had on him was tremendous. They had helped him so much, and he wanted to let other teens gain this insight into life. He did not want to see anyone get in a "dump truck accident" ever again. Research has shown that suicide is the second leading cause of death among persons aged 10–24 years in the United States. It accounted for 5,178 needless deaths in this age group in 2012, up from 4599 suicides the year his sister died.

The personal experience Dominic's family went through with the loss of his sister was too much. The people who take their lives may think they are better off. They believe they leave everything behind and escape from their problems, but the pain and problems they leave behind never go away. The problems just grow and find someone else to attach to.

Dominic knew someone else who had carried Nadia's burden, Angel Morales. He was the fire fighter that had delivered the message to his parents. Angel had come by the house once a year, around the anniversary of Nadia's death. He was young at the time of the accident, and that was his first fatality. He was touched by Nadia, her eyes, her smile, and her love for her family. Angel also felt that he had a special connection to Nadia. After all, he believed she had seen him as her King and confessed her sins to him, thinking he was an angel.

At least, that is what he had thought. Nadia was not that deep. Little did he know that she had just recognized him and his name from the 911 call the day before when he had responded to Miss Schwimmer's heart attack. When she said that he was her King, she meant like a homecoming king, not Christ the King. What he didn't know didn't hurt him. Besides, maybe it was God's way of helping Angel and the Baxters. It made them all feel like she had confessed her sins and was with God.

Dominic and his parents had grown close to Angel and he wanted to share his idea with him. Dominic went to the firehouse with plans in hand. By this time, Angel Morales was Lieutenant Morales and was actually just starting up a program of his own. It is called Youth on Fire. The program allows high school students to join and train as a junior firefighter. They wouldn't go on official calls, but students would have the opportunity to participate in the same training that actual firefighters go through. They will help follow up on people after emergencies to see how they are doing, collect donations, and make deliveries.

"I never want to see a child take their own life ever again. If I can get them involved with something that can make a difference, maybe they can feel a little pride and self-worth," Angel explains.

He hoped to help anyone who felt lost, depressed, or desperate. To show them how to lift themselves up, and improve their life instead of taking it.

"A person that takes their own life will spend eternity in hell," Angel states, "Death will not end their problems, but be the beginning of them."

"I can't speak to that," Dominic tells Angel, "But I know that we can help. Let's work together to get these programs kicked off."

"I'm sorry," Angel says. "I didn't mean to be insensitive. Nadia, she's fine," he insists. "She confessed her sin right before she said your name and smiled. She is with Him."

"Oh, no," Dominic assures him. "I'm not offended. It's just that there are a lot of different beliefs about the afterlife. Maybe we have to get it right before we can meet our Maker, and if we mess up, we have to be reborn and start all over again. Our new life may even be more difficult, kind of like purgatory."

"Like reincarnation?" Angel, being a devout Catholic, shakes his head, "Let's agree that whatever our afterlife holds for us, we need not get there early. There is too much to do here on this earth. Plenty of His work to be done."

"I agree," Dominic states. "Can you make it to dinner tonight, Angel? My treat."

"Well, as long as you're treating me, can we go somewhere special?"

Angel and Dominic meet that night at Savory and Sweet 16, a not-so-fancy sports bar known for its love of college basketball, savory burgers, and sweet desserts. It's the perfect place, a relaxed environment with great food. It's nice to get out, away from the same daily routine. Dominic and Angel talk about what's been going on in their lives. They share stories and laugh till they cry. Angel tells Dominic about his wife and their children and how he has become such a dad that they now own a minivan.

"I don't think I'll ever drive a minivan," Dominic ribs him a bit. "How do the guys at the station let you get away with that? Thought you had to be a man's man. Not a dad, man. You have to protect your image."

"Well, they don't know," he laughs at himself. "They will never see me drive that thing. I own a full-size dually black truck. And that's all they know."

They laugh and go on like this for a while. Watch the game and shoot the breeze.

"Well, we better talk about our programs," Dominic suggests.

"Ah, let's just visit some more. I haven't seen you in years. I've seen your parents, and they are so proud of you. Always bragging about you. Can't blame them. You've done pretty well for yourself. I want to know more about what's going on with you. Do you have a special someone in your life?"

"Not yet, no one special. I've just been focusing on school and my career."

Angel looks at Dominic and says, "You may want to think about sharing that brain and good looks with someone special one day."

"I am good on my own," Dominic says.

"You have so much to offer. There's someone special out there who can share your life with you know. You are always trying to help others. Let someone in," Angel says with a grin.

"Come on, let's grab a beer, get some quarters, and shoot some basketball on the arcade game," Dominic changes the subject.

"Alright, alright. We can talk business tomorrow. Come by at lunch, and we can hash out the details. Besides, I have a few good men that I know want to be involved," Angel says.

"Sounds good, now let me show you how to shoot some hoop, nothing but net," Dominic says as he lets the ball fly.

"Sounds like the fire alarm, you ringing that rim."

The two laugh and go on like this most of the night. They hash out the details of their venture together the next day at the firehouse. There's lots of planning and excitement. They are feeling good about the programs. Both of them have the gift of being a giver. There are many people out there who can use help and many teens who need to learn that they can and do make a difference in this world. Dominic and Angel are confident and excited that their programs will do just that.

Little did they know that one of the first groups to sign up had one particular teen who desperately needed help. His name is Aidan, and he is actually a student at Dominic's alma mater. Stratford High is still going strong. It is a great school for some but a torture chamber for others. For Aidan, it's the latter and his living condition is a pretty stark contrast to the home that Dominic and Nadia had grown up in.

# Chapter 9
# Aidan

I am jolted awake by the jackhammering outside my window. I cover my head with the covers, hoping to get a few more minutes of sleep. The banging of the jackhammer has a certain rhythm that, if I can get used to, maybe, just maybe, sleep a little longer. Just as I start to doze, the high-pitched beeping of dump trucks backs up. Argh...

I get up and walk to my door. I remove the chair that is propped under the doorknob. I shove it under the handle every night because the lock on my door doesn't work. It didn't take me long to figure that out. People can't just come in here whenever they want. This is my room, my safe space.

I hope my sister has not showered yet. If so, there'll be no hot water left for me. Yes! I pass her room and see that she is still in bed. I walk down the hallway, stepping over the dirty clothes that are strewn about. I turn on the shower, and the water trickles out. The pressure is low, as usual. The warm water drizzles on my head, and I have a flashback. I was around 11 years old, asleep in my bed, when my mom's boyfriend, Buster, came into my room. He pisses on me, saying that he is teaching me about life.

"You know, Aidan, sometimes in life, you are nothing but a little pissant. Now get up, clean yourself off, and go make me breakfast."

When I try to tell my mom what happened, she warns me that "snitches get stitches" and tells me how lucky I am that he gives a shit about me and is teaching me the ways of the world. I'm so lucky.

I snap out of it, wash off, and leave the shower. I pick up a towel off the ground and dry myself. It's a little damp, raggedy, and stinks. Wow! What a metaphor for my life. I wrap the towel around my waist and go to the kitchen. I open the refrigerator and am surprised to see leftover pizza. I don't know where it came from and don't care. I have something to eat.

I look around to make sure the coast is clear and stuff the whole piece of pizza in my mouth. It is intentional that I don't sit down to eat it or use a plate like polite society. If there is no proof that I ate it, I have plausible deniability. Maybe, whoever left it in their hungover stupor might forget it was there. No napkin, no plate, no witnesses, I did not eat it. And if accused, I will just start screaming and complaining about how there is never any food in the house and what kind of home this is. I'll say that I only go to school so I can eat. Free lunch at Stratford High, it's my favorite subject!

Sometimes I feel bad about how I treat my mom, but as her dickhead boyfriend taught me, "everyone gets shit on sometimes." God, I hate myself.

I go to my room and get dressed. Clean underwear, yes! It's my lucky day. My school shirt from yesterday is lying across my dresser. It is still good because I didn't have PE yesterday. Now I put on my uniform pants, well everyone knows that pants can be worn for weeks before needing to be washed.

I am thinking about skipping today, but that piece of pizza stimulated my appetite. It is my favorite cafeteria day, Taco Tuesday. I get dressed and leave home with my sister and mom still asleep in their rooms. I walk past the construction workers, the jackhammers relentlessly pounding on the street, the dump trucks moving about, and come to the realization that my mom and sister are actually passed out, not just sleeping.

"Dumb frucks," that's what I called them when I was little. My mom thought it was so funny and it kind of stuck. "Dumb frucks," that's what they are, waking me up like that, the dump trucks, not my mom and sis. But, now that I think about it, they are kind of dumb frucks also. I hate them.

It's ok, because, I hate myself too.

I walk to school, thinking of what could be. The what if's that never go answered. What if I had a mom and dad that actually worked a steady job? Or better yet, what if I had a dad who worked and a stay-at-home mom? Someone who made dinner and took care of me and my sis? Maybe she could go to my games, not that I play ball or anything. But what if I did? Maybe I could be the star player, scoring the winning basket, being admired by all in school.

"Hey Aidan," they would call out, "Nice shot! Great game! Whatcha doing later? Wanna hang?"

Wanna hang? Oh no, not the best choice of words for me. No, no, no, don't go there. Hang out. Wanna hang out is what I meant. Too late. The thought has entered my head, and I can't escape it. Wanna hang? Do I want to hang myself? Why yes? Yes, sometimes I do. It sure would be a lot easier than my day-to-day life. I wonder what it would be like. I imagine it would be jolting at first, but then maybe a warmth would run through my body. Warm, right up to my last breath. Or maybe not...my thoughts take a turn for the worse, in reality, it's probably not a good way to go.

Hanging there, convulsing, fighting to get free. And no circulation. I would be cold, not warm, you idiot. Too slow and painful, probably. Too many thoughts start racing through my head. My head, a gun, a gun to my head would be faster. My thoughts race and spew out of my head just like my brains would. I stop myself from thinking of all the gory details. It would be quick. I bet I could get a gun if I really wanted.

"Stop, Aidan, stop thinking about it," I tell myself.

My thoughts go off on a tangent. What if I did have a gun? Would I really try to kill myself? Could I do it? Maybe I could just use it on all the people who have made my life a living hell? Maybe, then, I could be happy and carefree. Maybe, then, I could lead the life I can only dream of.

No, it wouldn't work. I'd shoot all the assholes around me, and just when I started to enjoy my life, I'd come across even bigger assholes.

There are assholes everywhere you go, and I'm afraid that I will become the biggest of them all. Besides, I'd probably get caught. I'm kind of impulsive and not very smart. My mind races.

Hey, what do you know, at school already, Stratford Prep. The sight of school snaps me out of it for a bit. I head onto campus and keep my head down. I make it to the cafeteria, free breakfast, my second favorite subject. I head in and see one of my friends, BJ, and call out.

"Hey, what up?"

"Aidan," he says, "I thought you were skipping today?"

"Nah, it's Taco Tuesday, my man. Gotta get me some."

"Speaking of, you see the new girl?" BJ asks.

"No, where?"

"Don't bother. She's way out of your league, but she is something to look at. Right over there, sitting with the ever so popular, Tamara."

"Awe man, Tamara's got her claws in her already? What's a guy gotta do?"

"What you doing after school?" BJ asks.

"Nothing, man, what's up? Wanna hang?" I ask.

A not-so-great image flashes through my head, cold and convulsing. Awe, man, I think to myself, I gotta stop using that expression.

"Yeah, I got this new video game, AWW, Apocalyptic World War. You gotta come check it out. It's so cool."

BJ sees someone he's been waiting for, "Hey, gotta run. See you after school?"

He gets up and rushes off.

"Sure," I reply, and "Sure, I got your plate," I mumble under my breath. I finish breakfast and drink my chocolate milk in a bag, which is so weird. I get up, grab my plate and BJ's plate, and head to the garbage cans.

"I see you are practicing for your future career as a janitor," Tamara says snidely. She turns to the rest of her table and laughs.

I hate that girl. Like I said earlier, a gun is not a good idea. I might use it.

My dark thoughts quickly turn into a chuckle when I turn around. There's some girl walking around carrying two milk bags. She is holding them up, close to her chest, walking around offering them to anyone interested.

"Want some?" she would ask and jiggle them around.

I don't know whose idea it was to put milk in a plastic bag, but it sure has cheered me up.

"I want 'em."

"I bet you do," she says, laughs and hands me both bags.

Thanks to the extra milk, I survived the morning. Sleep most of the time, but I make it to lunch. Taco Tuesday is my favorite. I eat my tacos and split. I can't take school anymore today, so I head out the back alley and walk to town.

I keep a low profile so as not to draw attention to myself. I'm pretty much invisible, so I don't expect to get caught. What could they do to me anyway? Write me up for skipping. Whatever? Just keep a low profile.

I roam the streets looking for something to do. I walk by the river and skip some rocks. Skipping. Ha, skipping rocks while skipping school. Man, I'm the King.

I sit down and look up. I see this little tugboat pushing these gigantic ships. How does that little tug move that big old ship? Seems like too much. His engine should overheat or just blow up, lose his cool. I don't know, with all the pressure and shit I have to carry, sometimes I just want to explode. I admire the little guy for a while longer before I realize so much time has passed. School has been out for at least an hour now.

Blow up, explode. Awe man, I was supposed to go to BJ's. He got a new video game. I could be killing something. A good way to escape my thoughts for a while. Plus, I get to blow stuff up.

Maybe I can just meet BJ at his house. I get up quickly and turn to go.

"Excuse me," a person says as she dodges to the right to get out of my way. It's the new girl from school. I almost walked right into her. I could feel the blood rush to my face.

"I'm so sorry," she said.

"My fault," I lower my head and walk away, but she keeps talking.

"Didn't I see you in school today, Stratford Prep? Today was my first day. I just started there. I'm Catarina."

"Ah, yeah," I mumbled and kept walking. "Future janitor, that's me," I thought and ran off.

I walked all the way to BJ's, disgusted with myself. She is beautiful AND was talking to me. Catarina, what a pretty name. She started the conversation. What the heck is wrong with me? "My fault, and ah yeah," that's what you said! So cool, smooth, and cool under pressure. Not! I'm not like that tugboat at all. I can't handle anything. I'm more like a dump truck, making all kinds of racket and dumping shit all around. What a Dumb Fruck I am!

I ditch BJ's and head home. Can't take being around people anymore. Home is not the best place to be, but if I can just get to my room. No one's home, thank God for small favors. I go to my room, shove the chair under the doorknob, and crank up the radio to drown out the sounds of street repair outside and the sounds in my head. I lie on my bed and listen to the music coming from the speakers. I can even feel the vibration. I like rock. It helps drown out everything.

Once the music takes over and my thoughts stop racing, I close my eyes and sleep, my great escape.

My nap doesn't last long. My sister and mother come home making all kinds of noise.

"Aidan, where are you? Get up! Come see!"

I turn over and cover my head with the pillow.

"Come on, come see! We have a surprise," my sister bangs on my door. "Come on, we are eating like royalty tonight."

"Eating like royalty," I thought, "I can do that!"

I get up and sleepily walk into the kitchen. It's a nice surprise and a happy setting, days of old come flooding back. When we were little, nothing seemed too bad. My sister and I loved to laugh and play. It didn't matter if we didn't have lots. We had each other. We had my mom then, too. That was before she began dating Buster and self-medicating. She had us, and we were enough.

"What's the big deal?" I ask.

"Well, someone else's emergency has become our blessing. I was about to end my shift when, the table I was serving got a phone call. They had a family emergency and had to leave. I think it was a good emergency, like someone went into labor and was about to deliver. They paid the bill and left all of the food, a table of food for six. Well, I packed it up, and here it is! Plus, the guy threw two $100 dollar bills on the table and told me to keep the change. God bless that man and his family."

"And Buster?" I said aloud, but "Ball buster" is what I think. "Is he on his way?"

I didn't want to get too excited if he was coming. He would take everything for himself and leave us the scraps, or he would eat all the main course and give us the sides. Asshole.

"He's not coming," my mom said. "He will be out of town for a while."

"Yes!" I thought to myself. It is a true blessing, my sister brought home tons of delicious food, and the ball buster is out of town. I hope it's like when my dad went out of town and never came back. Buster never coming back would be awesome, the best thing ever.

We sit and eat. The man had ordered steak, the mom had grilled tuna, and the children had a mixture of things: spaghetti, chicken strips, a cheeseburger, and a hamburger. We all took a taste of each meal, weird combinations, but so good.

"You can have the steak," my mom said. "You are the man of the house tonight."

After stuffing our bellies, we sat and watched TV for the rest of the evening. It was a great evening. Maybe we can have more like these. I can deal with this.

The next morning started off with a bang. Lots of banging. Ah, the sounds of the city. The jackhammering had started again. The beeping from the dump trucks backing up. Never liked those damn things, don't know why. Maybe because people made fun of how I pronounced it, dumb fruck. That's what I would say when I was a kid. Now, they are the bane of my existence. Hounding me every day with their freaking noises, back up beeping like an alarm going off.

The call of the dumb fruck,

Beeeep, beeeeep, beeeep... Here I am.

Beep, beep, beep, fill me up.

Beep, beep, carry shit around.

Beep, beep, beep, dump on someone.

Beep, beep, beep, repeat.

That's all it does. Carry and dump. I can relate to that truck. Sometimes, I feel all the weight of the world and have to lighten my load by dumping it on someone else. Or, if I get something good to carry around, I can't keep it, I have to go give it to someone else.

Sometimes, I am the victim of the fruckers, being dumped on. Never is it taking away my crap. It's always dumping on me. It's smothering. I hate dump trucks, always have.

"Wait," I think, "Snap out of it. There are leftovers in the fridge."

I get up with a little spring in my step. Food in the fridge and no Buster. Today's going to be a good day. No heavy load to carry today.

# Chapter 10
# Youth On Fire

"Hey loser," BJ calls out as I walk into school. "What happened yesterday?"

"I'm sorry, man. I had to get out of here. I went to the river and kinda got lost in my own world. I was going to head to your house until I ran into the new girl."

"What?"

"Yeah, I ran into the new girl, literally. It was humiliating. I was sitting by the river, just chillin', and when I remembered, I was supposed to meet you. I hurried to get up and take off and almost ran her over."

"Did you actually run into her? Probably the closest you will ever get to feeling her up," laughed BJ.

"Ha, ha, very funny," I said. "Probably right," I thought.

"We have a guest speaker today," BJ reminds me.

"What for? To talk about bullying? We know all about it. Experience it every day," I mock.

The first bell rings, and we head to first period. Roll is called, and then off to the gym. There is a firetruck sitting in the parking lot.

"What's going on?" I wonder. "Is there an emergency? Is someone hurt or sick? Maybe Ole Miss Schwimmer finally 'retired.'"

I look at the fire engine and realize that it is there for the meeting. It has a sign hanging on it that says…"Youth on Fire."

Fire, that would be a horrible way to die. Maybe an explosion that would kill everyone instantly, then it wouldn't matter if we burned up. I can see the headlines now, "Tragedy at Stratford Prep, Suicide Bomber."

"Why would anyone do that?" people would ask themselves and each other. They know why, just don't want to admit it.

Such a tragedy, they would say. Well, the tragedy started way before that and it occurs daily. Some of us live in our own little hell on earth. Not enough to eat, a neglectful mom and her abusive boyfriend, school bullies, and, let's not even get into the online stuff. Come on people, you were teenagers once. Maybe you were the Tamara, the popular girl, that has everything and made everyone else's life hell.

"Aidan, dude, hello? You there? What's up, man? Where do you go? You just kind of zone out," BJ laughs.

"Awe, man, I was just thinking how great it will be to have another adult telling me what to do, how awesome I am, and how great my life can be. Actually, you know what, I guess if they're going to tell me, today would be a good time because I'm in a pretty good mood.

My belly is full and Buster has been gone. Mom says he went out of town. Hope he stays gone."

"Well, it's a good day then," BJ says." Let's go have a listen, better than math class."

We get to the gym, and once everyone arrives, there is a low roar, people visiting and talking, laughter, and high-pitched squeals every so often. The principal gets on the microphone and quiets everyone down.

"Okay, boys and girls, ladies and gentlemen, we have some very special guest speakers today. I would like for you to give them your total attention. They are giving up their time to share some words of wisdom. Let's begin with a welcome for one of our very own, Mr. Dominic Baxter."

Dominic introduces himself as a proud graduate of Stratford High.

Not very interesting or relatable, I think to myself as he talks about his accomplishments. I'm not really interested until he gets further into his speech. He speaks of the tragedies that have occurred in life and the methods he has used to overcome them. His sister had taken her own life 16 years ago when he was only 8 years old.

Now you have my attention. The year I was born, I was arriving just as she was escaping.

He said that it was difficult, but it wasn't until around his senior year in school that some depression hit him. All he did was think about his problems, be envious of other people, and feel sorry for himself. Said he talked to himself often, "What's the point of life? Why is all this happening to me? What is wrong with me?"

He goes on to say that his parents did not want to ignore the warning signs and took action. They made him join Seniors Helping Seniors, a club that helps the elderly.

"It was either that or have no life at all. That was the option they gave me, no car, no phone, no going out, no nothing. This club was the start I needed," Mr. Baxter continues.

"It connected me with people out there that really needed help. Their problems seemed to help place my thoughts into perspective. I often felt helpless, but then I would go to the home of this elderly couple, the Sassos. Man, they were bad off. The gentleman used a walker but could still barely get around. The wife was better, but not much. How would they even live without the assistance of others? This helped me realize that I was not so bad off. Even though there were a lot of things beyond my control, I could walk and fend for myself."

"As a teenager, you may feel stuck following so many rules. Feeling that you just wish you were grown so you could do what you want. Well, through volunteering, I realized that no matter your age, problems persist, and limitations are always present. The way to fix them is to do something. Do something that you can control. Do for others what they cannot do for themselves. It will come back to you."

This Dominic guy had grabbed my attention, and apparently everyone else's too. It was so quiet in the gym.

"It changed my life," Dominic professes. "Those few hours and those wonderful people, God rest their souls, really helped me. The attitude I had learned with the Sassos began seeping out into my everyday life. I began to be more attentive and helpful to others and for some reason, just happier, more content. I had a purpose."

"Mr. Sasso had explained it to me. Once we start focusing on others, he said, we can see that our problems are sometimes smaller than we think. Taken on their own, our problems are tremendous, paralyzing even, but when put into context of all that is going on in the world, they seem to fit. They are more manageable. Times still get tough, and worries and doubts always creep in, but there is a time and place to worry about everything. You don't have to carry your issues everywhere, every minute of the day."

I think about my analogy of the dump truck. Maybe this guy actually gets it.

"That's what I am doing here," Dominic exclaims. "I want to offer you an opportunity to DO. My law firm has started a non-profit to encourage people to DO, Donate Oneself. There are many opportunities and ways you can DO. Stop focusing on yourself and do something. You can help a neighbor, cut their grass, babysit, go shopping for those who are homebound, or tutor a younger student."

"You can give some time to the Senior Center or the retirement home. There is so much we can learn from our elders. Be a candy striper, rock new born babies. There are so many opportunities to help others. And trust me, it will come back to you. If you help others, you will be helping yourself in a way you cannot imagine. That's what it's all about."

"I have something to do," BJ turns to me and laughs. "I have tanks to go home and blow up on my new video game."

Apparently, Dominic's speech did not catch BJ's attention as it had caught mine.

Dominic continues, "Now, the fire truck is here because it is one of the new programs we are promoting. The fire department has a new youth training program available to you. It is run by Lieutenant Angel Morales and is called Youth on Fire."

Lieutenant Morales steps up and nods, "Good morning, stay with us," he joked, thinking back to how these lectures always made him fall asleep when he was in high school. "Open your eyes. Come on, you can do it."

I look around and see students lift their heads and sit up a little straighter. He was right, lots of students had started dozing off.

"We aren't finished here yet. You have so much to do and so much to learn," Angel says. "We are almost finished and will have you out of here in no time."

Whoa...serious déjà vu! His words echo in my head. I feel as if I have heard this before. So weird, I hate it when that happens. I shake it off and continue to listen.

"But seriously," Lieutenant Morales continues, "let's talk about Youth on Fire. The program doesn't cost anything but some of your time. You will get to participate in active training, CPR, and search and rescue training, and you get to assist those in need who have recently had fires or medical emergencies. There are so many people out there who could use some assistance. And without even knowing it, in helping others, you will help yourself. That's what it's all about."

Dominic steps up again, "Whatever it is, we want you to DO! Your teachers will have a handout on the different volunteer opportunities and a special form from the Youth on Fire. Please look over them and consider participating. Remember, life is what you make it."

After the program, we head back to our classrooms. I see Dominic and Lieutenant Morales walking towards the fire truck. I jog over there and call out, "Mr. Baxter, excuse me, Dominic Baxter, Lieutenant Morales."

They still don't hear me, and I holler, "Hey, Dom!"

Hey Dom? Why would I call him that?

Dominic Baxter stops dead in his tracks and turns to me, "Dom? Well, I haven't had anyone call me that in years."

"I mean, Mr. Baxter," I correct myself.

"Please, it's Dominic. Mr. Baxter is my father. How can I help you?"

"Ah…., I…., well, I…" I couldn't even string two words together. What is wrong with me lately? Flabbergasted by the girl yesterday and can't speak now.

Dominic smiles and a warmth suddenly overcomes me, and I relax. "I want to join," I tell him.

"Your teachers have handouts to give you. Just call that number or come by the station one day. This is Angel Morales. He is in charge of Youth on Fire. We would love to see you there. Thanks for your interest."

I get back to class and wonder what just happened. Why did I have such a strong reaction to this? It's not like me. Lay low. Keep your head down. That's my motto. Pretty opposite of DO.

Class begins, and Tamara begins running her mouth about how she already volunteers and her parents are donors to many worthy causes.

"Yeah, to your wardrobe," someone calls out. "They must donate a fortune to it."

"Some of us take pride in ourselves and how we dress." She stares at me as if to say, "And some of us don't."

Everyone reacts, and the teacher settles us down. She doesn't address what was said, she just moves on and tells us to open our books to pg. 123. Oh, how I just love school.

While sitting there, I think of Dom again. What is wrong with me? Why was I so drawn to this guy? Maybe he is the type of person I wish I could be or the role model I'd like to have in my life. I'm not sure, but I can't shake the presentation or presenter out of my head.

School drags on until, finally, the dismissal bell rings. I head outside and take a deep breath. Man, what a day.

"Wait up," I hear a voice calling out. I turn to see the new girl, Catarina, walking briskly towards me.

I look around. Is she talking to me? It can't be. I play it off and turn back around.

"Hey, wait up. Did I do something wrong?"

What? I turn around again. She is talking to me. I wait for her to catch up.

"Ah, yeah," I mumble, "I mean, no."

"Hi," she says. "Do you mind if I walk with you? You live by the river, right? I remember running into you there," she giggles a little. "I'm new here and don't really know anyone. Mind if I walk with you?"

"Um, no problem. Sorry again about yesterday."

We walk a few steps.

"Are you sure you want to be seen with me? I'm not the most popular guy. May not want to be seen with the future janitor."

## Surviving Sixteen

"Oh, stop," she says. "I can't stand those types of girls. That girl, Tamara, I'd rather her NOT want to be friends with me. I can't stand being fake. I would have to miss out on opportunities like this, walking home with Stratford's future janitor."

What? Man, I can't ever tell what girls are saying. I look at her. Does she mean walking with me? Is she insulting me or flirting? What is going on today? I think to myself. I chuckle a little. This beautiful new girl wants to walk with me. We're going to walk together from school all the way to the riverfront.

I don't dare tell her that I do not live by the river. We walk and talk. She's nice and talkative, which is good for me because I am kind of at a loss for words. Again, not the smoothest. I walk her to her door and she thanks me for the company.

"See you tomorrow," she says and goes into her house. And wow, what a beautiful home it is. It is one of those homes you see in a brochure. Why would she want to talk to me? Oh yeah, she thinks I live in this area too. Damn, why didn't I say something? Now I'm stuck pretending to be something I'm not.

I turn and walk another 30 minutes to my house, what a stark contrast to hers. The jackhammer is still going, dump trucks, loading up broken cement and taking it off. Workers hanging out watching other people work. I'll never understand why they have so many workers. It seems like there are always a couple of men working and lots of others just standing around watching. Reminds me of those lightbulb jokes:

"How many people does it take to screw in a light bulb?"

You know the ones.

"How many Tamaras does it take to change a lightbulb?"

"Just one. She holds the lightbulb, and the world revolves around her."

"How many therapists does it take to change a lightbulb?"

"None. The light bulb has to want to change."

Well, kind of like me right now. My mind goes back to the presentation from today. Do I want to change my life? Do I want to DO?

I don't know. I hate to get my hopes up just to have them crushed. Do I dare shine the light and examine who I am and what I can do with my life as Dom did, or do I stay in the dark?

I get home and eat some leftovers from last night's feast. The choice seems pretty easy. I go into my room, prop the chair against my door, and turn the lights out. Stay in the dark. This is my life, I am good at it. If I don't try, I won't fail. I fall asleep, satisfied with my decision.

"Where am I," I ask myself. "Am I awake or asleep? I know I laid down."

I am in such a deep sleep I cannot arouse myself. I am dreaming, but it's so strange. I want to wake up but can't. I am in a nice office, leather chairs in the waiting room, magazines with pictures of yachts and sports cars sit on the coffee table. I am in some kind of waiting room, but where?

"Ms. Baxter, Mr. Baxter will see you now," a lady calls out.

I look around. There is no Ms. Baxter there. There is no one but me in the waiting room.

"Excuse me, Miss? You may go in now," she repeats.

Me? Me? Is she talking to me? She is, she is talking to me. Wake up, wake up! I try my hardest, but my body will not wake. In fact, I stand up, thank the assistant and enter the office. What the heck? Wake up!

She called me Ms. Baxter. My thoughts go back to my dream. Mrs. Baxter, as Dominic Baxter's wife? Am I his wife? What is going on?

I enter the office and give Dom a hug and kiss. Nope, not his wife, not that kind of hug and kiss.

"I am so glad to see you. It's been so long?" Dom pours out his emotions. I think he's even tearing up. "I truly miss you. Things are just not the same without you around."

"Dom," I call out, and a single tear runs down my face.

In my dream, I appropriately reply, but I am trying to figure out what the heck is going on in my head. Dom and I sit and visit like old friends. My thoughts are still freaking out, not his wife, but am I a woman? Ms. Baxter? What is going on?

I look around for a mirror, none in sight. I try to look at my reflection in the window, but there is none. Let me correct that, there is a reflection, a reflection of everything, everything but me. I can see Dom, the plant, his desk, everything has a reflection but me! What is going on? Wake up, wake up, wake up! I try to rouse myself awake, but I can't. In fact, everything turns to black and hours pass until I wake the next morning with no memory of the dream.

# Chapter 11
# Opportunities

Bang, bang, bang, bang...the jackhammer noise wakes me bright and early. Beep, beep, beep, dumb frucks back up. Why do I even set my alarm? People pay top-notch for a wake-up service, but I have one free of charge right outside my window. I go through my miserable morning routine and end up at school in homeroom before I know it.

The teacher takes attendance as half the class visits with one another and the other half sleeps. High school definitely starts too early. Don't they know teenagers are night owls? Mrs. Williams begins doing typical morning business, picking up excuses or notes for the office, taking lunch count, and handing out any paperwork that should go home. Flyers are being passed out today. Don't they know we just throw this stuff away? Why are they still killing so many trees? Haven't they heard of email? Oh, wait! This is DO and Youth on Fire. Good thing it wasn't just an email, or I would have just marked it spam.

Oh wait, wait, wait, wait! Now, I'm really freaking out. Did I dream that I was a woman last night, went to see Dom and gave him a hug and a kiss? Oh no, no, no, no! The memory comes flooding in. Oh my, what does this even mean?

"Mrs. Williams, can I go to the bathroom?" I call out.

"Can you raise your hand and ask?"

I raise my hand and plead, "Can I please go to the bathroom?"

"I do not know," she mocks, "Can you?"

I correct my speech to "may I be excused" as I get up and begin to head out. I don't have time for this play on words, and I think I am going to hyperventilate.

I did. I did. I did. I was a girl, I had a dream last night, and I was a girl! I visited Dominic. Called him Dom again. Gave him a hug and a kiss! What the hell is wrong with me? I was a girl! I wash my face off and look in the mirror. I'm definitely me and definitely a male. What the heck? No reflection! In my dream, I couldn't see my reflection. My mind races, and I get a little lightheaded.

BJ walks in a few minutes behind me.

"You okay? Mrs. Williams sent me to check on you."

"Yeah, sure. Just needed some air."

There was no way in hell I was going to tell anyone what had happened.

We went back to class, and I made it through morning classes without freaking out again. It's finally lunchtime. I don't even enjoy my favorite subject today. I am still weirded out by that dream. I stay in a fugue state the rest of the day. The final bell rings, and I head out as quickly as I can.

"Well, I thought maybe you would wait for me today, but no, I have to practically run to catch up with you. I didn't think I was that bad of company," Catarina rambles on.

I can't do this now, I think to myself. I need to get home and chill and do manly things.

"Oh, I am not headed home today," I lie to her. "Sorry, I have to go see my mom at work today. Her office is in the opposite direction. Maybe tomorrow?"

Is it really a lie if my mom's main job is being home doing nothing? Technically, it would be her office if being a mom was her only job. Too bad she is not very good at it. What am I doing? I just passed up walking and talking with a beautiful girl to go home and do nothing. Why do I even exist?

"Okay, see you tomorrow," Catarina says. "Are you okay?" She asks.

"Yes, I'm fine," I reply, "just a little tired today. I'll see you tomorrow."

I head home, go to my room, prop the chair against my door, and crank up some rock music. I begin unpacking my backpack and come across the DO and Youth on Fire handouts. I rip them up without a thought. They should have emailed it and saved some trees. Yes! Back to my old self. Maybe BJ's home. I need to shoot something, blow something up!

I walk over to BJ's and get my fill of violence. It's nice to blow off some steam. My mind forgets about the day and the nightmare. Shoot, kill, die. Game over, start over. BJ and I play until the night. His mom finally makes it home with pizza.

"Want to eat?" she asks.

"Yes, Ma'am!" I think to myself how lucky I've been lately. Dinner three nights in a row, walking with a beautiful girl, and no Ball Buster in sight. Sweet!

"You can stay the night if you like. BJ, give him some clothes, and I can wash your uniforms for school," BJ's mom takes charge.

"Hell yeah! I've hit the lottery," I think to myself.

After we eat, BJ gets me a change of clothes and offers me a shower.

A real shower with real water pressure. This is the life. Things are looking up. I take a long, hot shower and think of Catarina. She is so pretty, and I can watch her talk all day. It doesn't really matter what she's saying. Her expressions are mesmerizing. Her eyes smile, and her lips… I begin to fantasize. Awe, man, I remember where I am. I stop myself and change to a cold shower.

The next day, I am awakened by the smell of pancakes. This is the life. Maybe this is what things can be like for me. I need to get out of that shithole I live in. I can't take it anymore, especially if Buster comes back.

## Surviving Sixteen

I eat breakfast with BJ and his family. He doesn't even know how good he's got it. I've heard him complain about his mom and dad, how they hound him and keep tabs on him. He has no clue. My mom didn't even look for me last night. She probably did not even know I wasn't home. Guess we all have our own problems.

"I received an email from your school yesterday," BJ's mom states. "It talked about some volunteer opportunities for you guys. Two strong, healthy young men like yourselves, you boys, should do the Youth on Fire. Sounds fun. Besides, BJ, you need to do something besides play video games. That's all you do. Life is more than that."

"But I like my life," BJ answers back.

"Not for long, if you don't join one of those programs," his dad implies that BJ does not have much of a choice.

We finish eating breakfast and head to school.

"You see what I mean? They always up in my grill. Why can't they leave me alone? They always preach to me, 'Treat others like you want to be treated,' they say. Well, that's what I do. I leave people alone so that they can leave me alone. That's how I want to be treated. Well, it doesn't work. They always want more from me!"

"Yeah, I get it," I lie. "You know, I actually thought about joining Youth on Fire. It might be fun. Better than being at my house. Maybe I'll join with you."

"Okay," BJ says. "Let's do it. Maybe it will be okay if we join together."

We get to school and go our separate ways. BJ has some honor's classes, and I struggle to just make it through mine. I think my life would be easier if I were smarter. It seems so much easier for everyone else. I don't know. Ole Miss Schwimmer always asks me if I used up all my intelligence in another lifetime or did I have any left for this life as if I would want to use it for her stupid class anyway. She's a mean old lady and hates everyone. I don't even get why she is a teacher. Someone asked her once why she became a teacher. She said that she was paying for the sins of her father. What the heck does that even mean? She's always saying weird stuff like that.

Anyway, I make it through all of my morning classes and get to lunch. Tamara and her groupies are hanging up posters for homecoming. I just don't get all that stuff. Homecoming court, let's reward all the popular kids and remind all of the losers that they are losers. High school is really good at one thing, letting you know where you stand. There are the athletes and cheerleaders, the nerds, the cool kids, and the losers.

Sometimes, I wonder what life would be like in one of those groups. What is it like for those guys? They all seem to have their own problems, yet have interests, friends, and purpose. I mean, I know the athletes and cheerleaders are always practicing and hanging out with each other. They seem pretty happy. Their biggest concern is who likes who and if they are going to win the game. The nerds, well, they are always worried about passing their tests or getting into a good college. They don't seem too happy but aren't really interested in happiness right now. It's like they know that they will make it to a good college and be everyone else's boss one day. That's when they will thrive. The cool kids, well, they don't seem to worry too much about anything.

They are pretty laid back and seem to be able to get along with pretty much anyone they want to. This is BJ. I don't think they worry too much about the future, past, or present too much. They just enjoy the time they are in. The losers, they are kind of outcasts, but they at least have each other. Me? Well, I think I am more of a loser and a loner. I do not have many friends, I'm not athletic, not too smart, and don't really want to be anywhere. I like to keep my head down and not get noticed. I wouldn't even mind if I didn't exist. Don't think anyone would miss me and think I even have much of a future.

I get my lunch and take it outside to eat. I cannot take all the excitement of those girls and their homecoming.

"Why are you way over here sitting by yourself?" I hear a sweet voice ask.

"Catarina. Hi," I reply.

"So, why are you sitting alone?" she asks again. "Want some company?"

I look up and smile a little. Still feel a little bad about lying to her and pretending to live by the riverfront.

"Sure, have a seat," I reply.

I don't feel that bad.

"Oh, I can't stand all of that homecoming stuff," she gripes.

No way, I thought to myself, "You should be the Queen. You are beautiful," is what I wanted to say, but "I thought that stuff would be right up your alley" is what came out of my mouth. Right away, I could tell by the look on her face that it was not the right thing to say.

"I told you; I don't like fake!" she exclaimed.

"No, I didn't mean it like that, it's just that, that," I hesitate.

"What?" she asks.

"Never mind," I mumble.

She sits next to me and begins to eat her lunch and unlike herself, doesn't say another word. The silence is painful.

"Were you here for that presentation?" I ask.

"Which?" She still seems a little perturbed.

"The volunteer program. BJ's parents are making him join and he begged me to join with him, so I think I might."

"Which one are you going to do? Have you decided?" Catarina is interested and maybe less irritated.

"I think we are going to do the fireman thing."

"Firemen or fire person? Like, what if I want to join? Do I have to be a fireman, or could I be a fire woman?"

Guess she's still a little aggravated. I am glad I had just taken a bite of my burger because my mouth was full, and I didn't have to answer. I just kind of shrugged my shoulders and shook my head.

"I may join too," she chimes in excitedly.

She's over it. Man, the mood swings with girls. I just don't get it.

"When does it begin? Where is it? How long does it last? Did you guys turn the form in yet? Do you have an extra one? I am so excited. Who is BJ, by the way? I don't think I met him."

She talks so fast, I think to myself. I don't even have time to answer. I just sit there listening and watch her speak.

"Would BJ care if I went with you guys? I haven't met him. Is he your friend? Did you grow up together? I have friends all over the country. My dad travels a lot with his job, and we go where the work is. This is my fourth school. It's not too bad. We don't usually move during the middle of the school year, and I make friends easily. I'm not very shy."

She goes on like this until the bell rings to end lunch.

"Well, great then, it's settled. I'll join you guys, and we can all be young fire people, or whatever you call it. I'll see you after school."

Catarina gets up and walks off. I don't say a word, but I wonder why she wants to hang out with me. Don't think she really knows me like I know myself. I don't even want to be around me. I look up and around, which I rarely do. Keep your head down, I think, but I can't help myself. If only I could be like anyone else. It seems like so many people have it better than I do. These last couple of days have just been a tease as to what my life will never be.

I have been taught from a young age that I will never amount to much. When life gives you lemons, well, you are the lemon, and it won't end well for you. They are going to squeeze every little drop out of you, mix you with water and lots of sugar to fix you up because you are not good enough. You will then be sold for a profit, be used to quench someone else's thirst, and once they are done with you, you will be churned in acid and pissed out. Down you'll go, flushed down the commode like the little piece of shit you are.

Buster, he has taught me so well, and my mother right behind him, thanking him for teaching me the ways of the world. If only I could be in someone else's shoes. I can be the one to make lemonade out of lemons. I guess we all have our place in the world. I'm about done with mine.

The people around me disappear into the buildings. They have all taken off and are headed to afternoon classes. I just sit here wishing I could disappear. Just be gone, or maybe go out with a bang. Let everyone wonder, what was that? I would project out all my thoughts and anger in one big bang. Look over here, and then, when they look, there will be nothing there. I would be gone. Nothing left. No person, no body, no doubts, no thought, no nothing. Wish I could go out with a bang.

The second bell rings, and it snaps me out of the dreadful thoughts.

"Mr. Aidan," principal Walker says as he pauses his walk. "I'm headed to my office. Would you like to come? I mean, if you have nowhere else to be, you can come with me. I am sure we can figure it out."

"No, sir. Sorry, sir, I'm going. My backpack spilled, and I was just trying to hurry up and get to class."

I fumble with my backpack, pretending to straighten up all of my things.

"Get going," he says and walks away.

That's exactly what I was thinking, although not quite like you mean it, I think to myself. Going out of school, gone away from here.

I get up and throw away the trash from lunch, a flash of my future. I can see it now, 60 years old, still in high school, walking around after all of the students head back to class. They walk right by me like I don't exist, and I begin picking up after all of them ungrateful little shits. Stratford High School Grounds Crew is what it says on my name tag. Janitor is what I am, watching, working and always cleaning up after others. Never a part of any group, just on the outside looking in. Having to pick up the pieces of everyone else's joyful gatherings, never being a part of it.

I snap out of it and head to my next class. I walk in late, and everyone looks at me. Their stares piss me off. Oh, now you see me? I get written up for being tardy again.

"There will be Saturday detention. Come get your slip," my teacher says as she shakes her head.

I grab the slip and slump down on my desk. I had a couple of good days I think to myself, now back to reality. I make it through the rest of the day without incident. As I walk out of the building, I hear Catarina calling my name. No one ever calls my name, at least not in the tone that she is. It is usually called out in disgust, "Aidan, come with me. Aidan, Saturday detention. Aidan, pay attention, Aidan, how are you ever going to make it in this world?" Not this time. This sounded different.

"Aidan," a sweet-sounding voice calls out.

I look up. It is Catarina. She is standing there with BJ. I walk up to them.

"Hey, I found BJ. Wasn't that hard," she says. "He is the only BJ at our school. I was telling him that I was going to join you two and be a fire person. I'm so excited. He said the first meeting is this Saturday. Let's meet at the coffee shop, then go there together. Okay? I'm so excited."

Man, the girl can talk, I think to myself.

"Yall are going to have to go without me, Saturday detention."

"Man, what's up with that? What happened?" BJ asks. "What about Youth on Fire?"

"I don't know. Maybe I can come by after detention. Not sure I really want to do it anyway. Maybe it's a sign that I shouldn't even do it."

"Oh, you're going to do it," Catarina declares. "Don't even think about backing out. BJ and I will meet at the coffee house, right BJ? While you are enjoying your detention, we will then go to the firehouse and sign all three of us up, and then you can meet us there. I'm so excited."

BJ and I look at each other and then again at her. We shake our heads as if to say okay. What other choice do we have? She has said it with such confidence that we just agree with her. Her hair and lips move at a rhythm that entrances us both. She is so pretty, of course, we are going to go. Whatever you say, Catarina.

# Chapter 12
# Missed Opportunities

Saturday morning arrives, and the realization that my actual alarm clock woke me up instead of the banging of the jackhammering sets in. This is just another reminder of the luck I have. A day I could have slept in without so much racket, I have to get up and go to Saturday morning detention, 7:30 am till 10 am. Who decides this, and why do they want to torture us?

I get in the shower and loathe myself. The water pressure is good today, but instead of feeling good, I feel the pressure of the drops hitting me. Each one pounds on me as the drops hit my head, but it feels like the same drop repeatedly hitting me. Loser, loser, loser, you can't do anything right. You have to go to detention because you're a dumb shit. Others drops pound on my body. Look at this, here, here, and here, you can't compare. You're weak.

I turn the shower off. Thanks for the pressure, I think to myself as I get dressed, grab my stuff, and head to the door. I start to open the front door to leave when I hear a groan that brings an instant pit to my stomach. I quietly turn and look. Buster is asleep on the sofa. Great, just great. No dumb fruck shortage today. I thought I was getting a break. I hang my head and walk in a trance-like state to school, partly because it's 7:30 in the morning and partly because Buster is back. I really hoped he would stay gone.

Detention drags on but finally comes to an end. Youth on Fire, I think about it. I don't have Catarina or BJ's parents telling me to go, and I wonder to myself why I agreed to join in the first place. I think I'll just skip it and go home. A flash of Buster crosses my mind and it quickly changes my mind. I decide Youth on Fire is the better choice.

I arrive at the firehouse and can see the program has begun. I see Catarina and BJ in the group. I stand back and watch for a while. I hang my head, turn to leave and bump into someone. It's Dominic Baxter, the presenter who came to our school.

"Hi," he said. "Do you need anything? What are you doing out here? Let's get you in there. Remember, it's always better to DO than to stand around watching the world go by."

"Ah, yeah, I just arrived," I stumble to get my words out.

The dread, like a fog I had been feeling all day, has just lifted. I follow Dominic into someone's office and see our reflection in the window. Oh man, I just remember that dream I had about him. Oh man, I'm so weird. At least this time, I'm actually me, not some girl visiting him in his office, giving out hugs and kisses. So, freaking weird.

Angel Morales walks into the office.

"Hi there. You are the young man I have been looking for? Your friends told me that you would be coming late."

"Yes, sir. Sorry. I had somewhere to be this morning," I reply.

"Well, I'm just glad you made it," Angel comments as he looks up. He hands me my nametag and a black marker. It's just one of those, hello, my name is, stickers. I write my name in all caps, AIDAN, and I stick it onto my shirt.

"You have so much to do and so much to learn," Lieutenant Morales says as he looks out through the window and motions toward the rest of the Youth on Fire crew.

Whoa, déjà vu. The room seems to slow for a minute. Everything is moving in slow motion.

"You with us? Come on.' Lieutenant Morales prods at me.

"No, I'm done. I am tired and just want to sleep now," my thoughts seem to echo in my head, or did I just say that aloud? Why would I even say that? Maybe it was just in my head. What is wrong with me?

Snap out of it! I tell myself and shake my head. I seriously need to consider medication. I feel like I am going crazy lately. Everything is moving in slow motion until I hear Lieutenant Morales shuffle some papers. The noise brings me back to the present.

"Alright then, Aidan, head on out and jump right in. They are waiting for you. The world is your oyster." Dominic's voice seems to break through the strange moment, and I feel a little better.

"Yes, sir," I reply and head out to join the crew.

I walk out and close the door behind me. I pause to collect my thoughts and can hear them talking to one another.

"That young man," Dominic says to Angel, then pauses for a long time. "Never mind, I'm just, uhh…" he hesitates, "glad he made it."

"Yeah, I think I know what you mean. There's just something about him."

Angel agrees with Dominic, and they shuffle around for a minute, feeling a little uncomfortable.

"Just something oddly familiar," Dominic says aloud, kind of to Angel, kind of just out to the universe.

"You know, I saw the reflection of his nametag in the window. It gave me pause."

"Why?" Dominic asks.

"His name is AIDAN, the reflection, it said NADIA, made me think of your sister. He has her eyes, too."

"Whoa," Dominic said, remembering, "I just had a dream the other night that she came to visit me at work. I know she is gone and has been for 16 years, but sometimes, I feel she is still with me. I guess this is just another sign that she is."

"Yeah," Angel said. She sure loved you. I will never forget how she smiled when she said your name, Dom."

I shake my head and walk away. I look up and see Catarina and BJ. It looks like they have become pretty good friends, not that I expected anything differently. Catarina is just the type of girl who can make friends anywhere she goes.

"Yay! So glad you're here. Let me tell you what we have done so far. We had to..." Catarina continues, and I hear her talking, but it's kind of more like a distant echo. Her flowing hair and the rhythm of her lips have entranced me again.

"Welcome," a firefighter acknowledges me. "We are about to do an obstacle course that would mimic certain movements that we, as firefighters, have to be able to do quickly. When we come across an obstacle, we want our reaction to be quick and natural. No hesitation. So, we practice. Can I get a volunteer to help me demonstrate?" the fireman asks.

BJ steps forward to volunteer and looks back at Catarina and me.

They go through the different parts of the obstacle course, stepping over some things and under others. Climb through a tunnel, up a rope ladder, and walk across a two-by-four, kind of like a balance beam with a pit of foam underneath, just in case you fall.

"The foam is not there in real life," the fireman jokes.

Once they make it across the two-by-four, they actually jump into the pit of foam and have to sort of swim their way back to the other side.

"Good job, BJ," the fireman reads BJ's nametag. "Thank you for your help. Now, we will all have a walk-through to practice, then, we will go through the obstacle at full speed. You will keep a record of your times and you will see that, with practice, you will get more confident and competent. Lives will depend on you. So, let's get started."

Each of us takes our turn to walk through the obstacle the first time. The second time through, we are told to complete it as quickly as possible. I am so glad I did not go first because I realized that the rope ladder is tricky at quick speeds.

The first kid who tried to do the course quickly must have fallen off that thing at least three times. And you sure look funny falling off the two-by-four into the foam pit. The foam kind of swallows you alive. At least the guy that fell laughed it off and made everyone laugh with him. I wish I could laugh things off like that. I imagined that if it were me, I would have been laughed at instead of laughed with. So, when it was my turn, I was sure to move with caution. I sure didn't want to make a fool of myself and get laughed at.

We trained like this for a while and then went into a classroom where we were given statistics on house fires. It was a pretty good experience. Even the classroom discussion was interesting, not like Ole Mrs. Schwimmer's lectures.

We are dismissed, and I am glad I decided to go, but now I dread going home.

"Want me to walk you home, Catarina?"

"Well," she hesitates, "BJ and I are going to get lunch. Do you want to come?"

"Yeah," BJ chimes in, "come with us."

"I can't," I reply. "I forgot, my mom needed me to help her with something. I'll see you guys on Monday."

There's no way I am going to accept a pity invite. Surely, that's what it was. They hadn't mentioned it before. Plus, I don't have money anyway.

What a shitty end to a fun day. Well, it was a shitty beginning too. Why would I expect anything else? I guess I had a glimpse of a good time during the training, but my real life always gets in my way. Why would I think it could last?

I head to the restroom before I leave, and BJ follows.

"What's wrong, man? Come with us."

"Nah, y'all have fun. Don't want to cramp your style."

"Man, it's not like that. If you like her, I'll back off. Do you like her? Cause I think we could, you know, hook up, unless you like her, then I'll back off. So, what's up, man? Wanna come with us? My treat?"

"No," I reply. "You go for it. She's pretty, but it's too much work to have a girl. You go for it."

"You sure man, cause, you know…" BJ grins.

"She's all yours if she will have your dumb ass," I laugh.

I look at BJ, and he has this goofy look on his face. He turns and jogs off. I hear him tell Catarina that I have to go help my mom and can't go with them.

I think that if only I could help my mom, I could have a better life. If she were normal and had a normal job and a normal boyfriend, I could be normal. But no, she is so unpredictable. Don't know if she will have a job or not. We may or may not have food at the house, and what's up with her choice of men?

There have been times when she really tries to do better, but it's like she is destined to fail. And thanks, Mom, you seem to have passed this quality onto me.

Let's just take today as a snippet of my life to examine this theory. First, I have to go to detention because I am a screw-up and have too many tardies. The one day the universe allows me to sleep in with no construction pounding outside my window, I have to get up early, only to go to detention, where I try to sleep but can't because I have to sit up straight and open a book. I don't have to really do anything with the book. I just sit there and assume the position.

"We give you the opportunity to be successful. What you do with your time is up to you, but you will assume an upright position and have a book open."

That's what they tell us. That's detention. So, what do I do, use my time wisely, better myself? No. I try to sleep sitting up. I get some rest, but it is not an easy task. So, I just sit and daydream, although it often feels like more of a nightmare. Detention is not good for my psyche. I just sit there and feel sorry for myself, then I get angry with myself and then angry with everyone around me. I don't want to be here, a common theme that runs through my brain. I don't want to be in detention. I don't want to be home. I don't want to be at Youth on Fire, although that actually turned out to be fun for a little bit. But right back at it, I don't want to go to lunch. I don't want to go home. I don't want to be anywhere. I don't want to be here. Like, I don't even want to exist.

Maybe I'll get sick and die, but with my luck, I would get some illness that would just cause me to live a long, painful life. I wouldn't even be able to die, just suffer. Or maybe I could get in an accident. Again, probably wouldn't work. I would probably just be paralyzed and have to depend on others. Who would even take care of me? I guess between my mom and sis, they would feed me enough to keep me alive and have me live a long, painful life.

I wonder if I could end my life and just start over. Maybe I could be a different person. Everyone else seems to be better off than me in some way or another. It couldn't be worse, right? Well, I guess it could be, but it's gotta be better than this. I think about if I took my own life, how would I do it? I always think of a rope, but I'd probably screw that up too. A gun, I don't think I could mess that up, but I don't even know how to get a gun. Maybe I could figure it out, but I'd have to get money first. Where would I get the money? Get a job? I don't think so. Loser.

I wash my face in the firehouse bath room and tell myself to snap out of it. "I'm done. I am tired and just want to sleep now" echoes in my head, and that's just what I plan to do. That was really strange earlier. Why did I want to say that to Lieutenant Morales earlier, too? I'm so weird. What's wrong with me? I walk home, go into my room and stick the chair under the door knob, my safe place.

I finally fall asleep and am quickly off to another world where life seems easier. Dom is there with me. We are riding around with the radio cranked up. I look in the mirror. Whew, I am still me, not some chic, this is good. How my thoughts and attitude quickly change in my dream state. I am happy to be alive and ready to take on the world. Dom and I spend the day going from place to place. We were at a ball field one minute and at the beach the next.

Dreams are strange like that. We are at a baseball game and get up and walk to the snack shack. We buy a snow cone, and when we turn around, we are on a beach. It's a beautiful day, and we walk along the water where the sand is packed by the waves. Little rocks freckle the sand. We visit and laugh, tell jokes, and talk about our dreams and goals. I can't really remember what we are saying from one minute to the next, but things are good. A feeling of fullness and satisfaction fills me.

We finish our snow cones and swim out into the ocean. I look around and suddenly cannot see anyone or anything else. The bright, sunny day turns to an eerie dark sky. The water is warm, and my eyes feel heavy. I close them for a long while and float. When I finally open my eyes a little, a slit of light comes shining through, and there is Lieutenant Morales in a lifeboat with an outstretched hand.

"Hang on," he says.

He grabs my wrist and tries to pull me in. I'm stuck. It's like something in the water is pulling me the other way. We are holding each other's wrists, but I can begin to feel our grasp slip. Whatever is under the water is pulling harder now and we lose each other. The water turns bitter cold. I start drifting further and further away. Lieutenant Morales paddles feverously towards me but does not seem to be getting any closer. He gets smaller and smaller. I close my eyes again, and blackness engulfs me.

I sit up in bed and take a deep breath. I think I had been holding my breath. For a second, I can remember flashes of my dream, but the longer I am awake, the more I forget it.

My thoughts are quickly interrupted by loud banging. Someone's here, I think to myself and go out to see who it was.

"Oh great," I mutter under my breath.

It's Buster and my mom. I walk into the living room to join them. Buster is going on about how he is going to be King and make it big. We have nothing more to worry about and will be able to get out of this dump.

"I got plans for us," he says as he grabs my mom around the waist. "I am going to take care of you. In fact, I am going to take care of you now."

He pushes his hips against hers, and she falls back into the wall. They start groping and kissing. That's my cue to leave.

I decide to walk to the river. I pass Catarina's house and wonder why I am so dumb. I should have gone with them to lunch. She is the one good thing in my life and she seems to like me, even invites me to lunch. What do I choose to do instead? Go home and go to sleep. What a loser. I get more and more angry at myself and then at the world.

I settle down for a bit and sit by the river. I start skipping rocks. I can't get them to skip too well because the water is rough. I start throwing the rocks as hard and as far as I can. My anger is so overwhelming. I feel warmth in my body that builds up and quickly turns into a heat that just irritates me even more. A fire burns within me. If I could only stay as cool as that little tug, but no, I may just explode. I am a youth on fire, I think to myself.

I run home, not knowing what to do with my thoughts and anger. Besides, what is Buster's big idea? What does he have planned? I am sure it is something that will ruin my life even more. I had a couple of good days, but the darkness is closing in again. I can't take it anymore.

I storm into my house and down the hall. The door to my mom's room is wide open and she and Buster lay naked on the bed. Really, can my life get any worse?

"Get your shit together and get rid of that loser," I scream out.

Neither of them budge. They are obviously passed out. Damn addicts, I think to myself, pitiful, disgusting, actually. I see a duffle bag lying next to the bed and grab it.

"What are you up to? What new living hell do you have planned for us?"

I go into my room, shove the chair under my doorknob, and crank up my music. I unzip the duffle and realize what Buster meant when he said he was king, a freaking drug king. The duffle was full of dime bags. I grab some and throw them across my room. I feel the rage building and grab another handful. I throw them too, and then, throw the whole damn bag across the room.

I hear something hard hit the wall. What else is in that bag? I pick up the duffle and reach inside. I feel something hard and cold.

"Hell yeah," I say as I grab what's inside.

It's exactly what I wanted, a gun, an answer to my problems.

Do something! I lift the gun to my head in an instant, all of the doubt, misery, and anger that had built up inside me, does it. IT pulls the trigger. A shot rings out, and in an instant, my lifeless body collapses to the ground.

I can't really remember anything real past that. It feels like I am dreaming again. I am engulfed by voices and colors, yet I feel nothing. Am I dreaming? I see a body that I cannot recognize lying halfway on the ground and halfway crumpled up against my bed.

A banging at my door. The chair keeps the door from opening. More banging.

"What the hell," I think to myself. "This is my room, my space. Go away."

My bedroom door starts to splinter and break in. Buster has kicked a hole in my door. He throws the chair out of the way and throws open my door. My mom, who has been screaming and crying out louder than the rock music, rushes in, stumbles over the dirty clothes on my floor, and falls onto the lifeless body.

"Aidan, no! Aidan," she screams. "No, no, no, no, no," her screams turn into a thunderous clap. The rock music is vibrating the room but her screams are louder. She grabs the bloody body. It slides away from her. She tries to lift it again.

"No, no, no, my baby," she cries out.

She tries to lift it again, still crying and screaming. It's too heavy, dead weight. She can't lift it. She lays on it and wraps her arms around it. She holds it tightly and rocks back and forth, screaming and crying out.

"No, no, no, no," she says repeatedly.

Buster tries to comfort her, but she is just hysterical. She pushes him away.

"Why? Oh, why?" She is screaming now. "It can't be, it's not him, it's not him, it's not," she repeats over and over as she feverishly rocks back and forth, back and forth.

Not who? I think to myself as I watch in horror.

She cries out my name again, "Oh Aidan, no Aidan, no!"

I suddenly realize what has happened. It's me. That is my body, my blood, my name she is calling out. What have I done?? Nothing seems real.

"I'm sorry. I'm so sorry. Mommy, I can take it back. I'm sorry, mommy. I know you do your best," I say to her in a childlike voice. She's not listening.

"I'll do better," I say. "I can change, Mom. I can, I can change my life. I want to change. I'll try harder," I plead.

She's still not hearing me.

"I'm sorry. I love you, Mommy. I'm so sorry. I'm sorry," I begin to cry.

"Get up, mom. Get up!" I demand. "It's not real. I'll do better. I'm sorry. Go back to sleep. When you wake up, it will be different."

She's not listening. Why won't she listen? This can't be real. I begin to cry harder. I haven't cried since I was a kid. My mom is holding me, sobbing, and now I am sobbing too. I feel things I haven't felt in years. The pain and sadness I feel is overwhelming. I try to go to her. I can't reach her.

"I'm so sorry," I manage to get out, sobbing so much I can barely speak.

She is getting further and further away. I desperately try to reach her.

"I'm so sorry," I whisper one last time and close my eyes. Everything goes black. I am drawn in. The blackness engulfs me. I am swallowed up.

# Chapter 13
# 911

Buster grabs the duffle bag and baggies that are strewn about and tosses them outside. He leaves the gun where it is. He grabs the phone and calls 911.

"We need help. Someone's been shot. I think he shot himself. The gun is lying beside him on the floor," Buster explains to the operator and proceeds to give the address.

Aidan's mom is still on the floor next to Aidan's body. She is shaking uncontrollably and sobbing. Buster gets a blanket, wraps her in it, and then sits and waits.

The noise of the sirens grows closer and closer. A fire truck is the first to arrive, followed by a couple of police cars and an ambulance. The firemen rush into the house and quickly realize that there is nothing they can do. They turn their attention to the mother, who is still sitting by the body, clearly in shock. They gently guide her away from the body and begin taking her vital signs.

"We are going to start an IV and give you a little something to help you relax," they tell her, but she doesn't reply. They continue to work on her and get her loaded into the ambulance and on her way to the hospital. She does not resist but does not seem to even know where she is or what is going on at this point.

## Surviving Sixteen

Police officers enter the home, begin securing the scene, and question Buster.

"I do not know where he could have gotten the gun," Buster lies. "He was a troubled kid. His father left when he was young. Has trouble in school, too. His mom does the best she can, but he was a handful," Buster elaborates.

"Can I get his full name?" the officer asks.

"Yes, it is Aidan, Aidan Samsara."

One of the firemen hears this and walks over to Buster, "Do you have a recent picture of him?" he thinks he knows the name, but the body is unrecognizable.

"Let me see," Buster pulls out his phone and pulls up a picture of Aidan.

The young fireman just hangs his head.

"That's him. That's the Aidan from today, from Youth on Fire. Oh, man. I just met this young man today," the young officer comments to Buster. "Just joined our program. Seemed like a great kid. Sorry for your loss."

The young fireman walked out of the apartment and approached his Lieutenant.

"Lieutenant Morales," he said. "That young man was one of our new recruits, Aidan Samsara."

Lieutenant Morales felt sick, just sick to his stomach. He and Dominic had just talked about this young man and how he had reminded them of Nadia. Now, he had taken his life, too? Lieutenant Morales stopped in his tracks, knelt down, and prayed for this young man's soul. He said a prayer for Nadia, too, while he was at it.

The next day, Angel called Dominic and asked him to come to the firehouse. He personally wanted to let him know about the call they had received last night. He could not have him finding out any other way.

Dominic entered Angel's office.

"Shut the door, will you please," Angel instructs Dominic.

"Sure, what's up?" Dominic asks.

Angel proceeds to inform Dominic about the call they got and how it looked like Aidan had taken his own life.

Dominic felt sick. He could hear Aidan call him Dom. It had just brought back memories of his sister Nadia, and now it brings this memory, the worst memory of all.

"He was gone in an instant," Angel says as if it will make Dominic feel better.

"I understand that, but it's every instant before that matters! Why do people do this? Why? Don't they know that they matter? Everything they do matters. They don't live in a vacuum. They leave a huge gaping hole in everyone else's life. Why are they so selfish?" Dominic breaks down and rambles on for quite some time.

"I would have done anything for her. In fact, I did. I made her laugh. We laughed. We played together, punch buggy, chase, and tag. I helped her with her chores. I would wash a million dishes to have her back. What is wrong with people? Don't they know they matter? They matter. They are just selfish, that's all. It could always be worse. Just look at where you are and add an illness to your situation. That would make it worse. Yes, it can be better, but it could be worse. Suck it up. Stop thinking of only yourself and start thinking of others. You think you have it bad. Look around people! There are many who have it way worse than you, and they make the best of it. What's wrong with you? Why would you leave me?"

Angel just listens. He has witnessed so much tragedy in his life and wishes he had the answers.

"Too bad we couldn't get a hold of that young man sooner. I think, if given the chance, he could turn his life around."

Silence fills the room.

"That is why we do this, Dominic," Angel continues. "Take some time and grieve. It brings flashbacks of your sister for me too. I can't even imagine how you feel."

Again, the two men sit in silence for a minute.

"We cannot give up either. We need to grow our outreach and keep doing God's work," Angel breaks the silence again.

"Why does God let such things happen?" Dominic snaps back, gets up and storms out.

"It is not our place to ask," Angel whispers.

A few days later, Dominic calls Angel and apologizes for blowing up. He also requests Angel to attend Aiden's funeral with him.

"Your involvement in our life after Nadia was a blessing. I just want to pay it forward. I would like to speak with the family. Let them know what we saw in him and maybe share my experience about my sister."

"Sure," Angel replies.

"I read his obituary and saw he had an older sister. I don't know, I've just been thinking of my sister a lot and how terrible it was for me. I feel like I lost her all over again. I just want to give a little support. Do you think that will be okay?" Dominic asks.

"I've been thinking of Nadia a lot, too," Angel replied. "Let's go to the service, and we will see how things go."

The two meet up and attend the funeral. It was a small service. Not many people were there, although they did recognize two attendees. It was the young man and young lady that signed him up for Youth on Fire. Dominic and Angel approach BJ and Catarina.

"Hello. We were so sorry to hear about your friend."

"Yeah," they reply in unison.

The four of them stand there in silence for some time, not really knowing what to say. Dominic looks around and sees Aidan's mom and sister, they are in the front by the coffin.

"You two take care," Dominic says as he approaches Ms. Samsara with hesitation.

Angel gently nudges Dominic forward and they both walk to the front and introduce themselves.

"Thank you for coming," Aidan's mom says and looks back down at the ground.

"And you are the sister? I'm so sorry for your loss," Angel acknowledges her.

"I could never know what you are experiencing and the feelings you are having," Dominic says, "but I have been in your shoes. I lost my sister in a similar circumstance. If you ever need to talk, reach out. I put my card in the back of the guest book. Call whenever you like."

The sister looks up but doesn't seem phased by his gesture.

The men stand there for a moment longer, then give their respects before walking away, "Sorry for your loss."

The two feel sad and inadequate, but what more can they do?

"That's all you can do for now," Angel tells Dominic.

As they reach the door, they hear a sweet voice call out, "We will see you on Saturday, Lieutenant Morales."

It was Catarina.

"Yes, you will," Angel answers, "YES, YOU WILL," he repeats as his heart fills with hope.

Angel turns to Dominic, "I know it is difficult, but we need to keep moving forward. We need to reach as many children as we can. This program is a good thing. It's too bad we didn't reach Aiden sooner."

# Chapter 14
# Outreach

Dominic lies in his bed that night and talks to himself, "I do make a difference. I must make a difference. There must be more that I can do to reach the kids that need me."

Dominic falls asleep and awakens with a new goal. He decides to "Do something," as Mr. Sasso had so wisely advised him. He starts advancing his career into a more specialized field. He begins representing children in juvenile and family court. He is very successful and works his way up to becoming the youngest judge to be appointed to serve as a juvenile court judge. He begins to feel a little more fulfilled and is helping lots of children in bad situations.

As the years pass, Dominic stays in contact with Angel, and they grow both their friendships and their organizations. DO is now a club in high schools nationwide, and Youth on Fire is expanding its program to neighboring communities. Youth on Fire also begins a program called Summer Hot Tots. It allows the teens from Youth on Fire to mentor a school-age child for a week-long summer camp. They teach the children basic fire safety and play games with them. It is a great success, allowing for more exposure and interest in Youth on Fire.

One day, a young couple walks into the firehouse.

"Is there a Lieutenant Morales here?" the young lady asked.

"No, but there is a Chief Morales at headquarters. He used to be the Lieutenant here years ago."

"That's got to be him," the young man looks at his wife.

"Can you please send him a message for us? We were in the first-ever Youth on Fire class sixteen years ago. He helped us through some difficult times. Helped us take charge of our future, and now we are entrusting our child to his program. We are signing her up for the summer camp."

"I sure will," the fireman replied. "What are your names?"

"I am BJ."

"And I'm Catarina."

"Got it. I'll send him the message. If you go ahead inside, someone will give you the forms to fill out for your daughter."

As they walk towards the office, the fire alarm goes off. The firehouse comes alive. It is a beautiful dance, the way the men and women get ready and head out. All the movements flow without a misstep, and in an instant, they are off with the roar of the engine and the sounds of the sirens.

"I admire what they do," Catarina comments to BJ.

BJ and Catarina kneel beside their daughter and watch the engines pull away.

"They are real heroes," they tell their daughter.

Once they can no longer see or hear the trucks, they enter the office and begin filling out the Hot Tot paperwork.

"This is where we started," Catarina explains to Julie, their daughter.

"This is the firehouse that your dad and I came to when we were in high school."

"Yes, I impressed your mom. I was the strongest and fastest guy here."

"Yeah, sure, that's what did it," Catarina laughs and stoops over and whispers in Julie's ear, "He was the sweetest and kindest boy here."

Catarina stands up again and adjusts her posture, "And even if he was the strongest and fastest guy here, he was still slower than me."

They both laugh, and Julie acts like it's the funniest thing she has ever heard.

There are pictures of each Youth on Fire graduation class posted on the far wall. They walk over to look at them.

"Look at mommy and daddy," Catarina points to their picture.

"Someone needs to be punished," Julie says.

"What?" her parents ask and look at her, filled with confusion.

"They didn't hang their clothes up or put their boots in the closet," she says, pointing at the picture.

BJ and Catarina look at each other. It is the tribute they had made for Aidan. It was a pair of training boots and a Youth on Fire Jacket on display.

"Oh," they kind of chuckled.

"Those are left there on purpose for a good friend, Aidan. He was not there to graduate with us, but he was a big part of our class, and we want him to be remembered," BJ explains.

"Who?" Julie inquires.

"His name was Aidan, and that story is for another day. Come on, let's go get something to eat," Catarina states.

As they turn to leave, they look up. There he is. It is Lieutenant Morales, well now, apparently, Chief Morales.

"Look who we have here," Chief Morales says. "If it isn't my two favorite youths on fire. How have you been?"

"Not as youthful anymore," Catarina laughs. "We are doing well. This is our little girl, Julie. She wants to join your program."

"I'm a Hot Tot!" Julie exclaims.

"Thanks for all you do and all you have done for us and the youth in our community," BJ says. "I will never forget all that you did for us."

155

"My pleasure," Chief Morales replies. "I think it helps me just as much. It has brought many smiles to my face."

"I know how to smile," Julie interjects. She is just as talkative as her mom ever was. "I have a princess smile. You have a hero's smile."

"You gotta love kids," Chief Morales looks down at Julie and gives her a big cheesy grin.

"There it is, a hero smile!" she exclaims and giggles.

Chief Morales smiles even bigger.

"Do you have a few minutes?" He turns back to BJ and Catarina, "I have a friend meeting me here, and I know he would love to see you two."

"Sure," they reply curiously.

"Oh, there he is. Come on."

They start walking towards someone but cannot quite make out who it is. The sun is at his back and he just looks like some shadowy figure.

Once they got closer, they recognized him.

"Hey, Dominic. It's great to see you again." BJ and Catarina say in unison.

"Oh, help me out with your names again," Dominic pleads.

"BJ and Catarina," they say one after the other.

"And I am a Hot Tot, Princess Julie."

"We were friends with Aidan," they timidly remind him.

"Yes, yes, I remember you guys well, just couldn't place your names. How have you been? And who is this beauty?" Dominic asks as he gestures toward Julie. "Does she belong to the two of you?"

"Man, some magic happened in this building," Angel brags.

They all laugh.

"It's true," Catarina says. "You guys have helped BJ and me through so much. We went through some trying times, but volunteering really did help us feel like we could make a difference. In fact, we named our daughter after a little girl we had met through your program. We often delivered clothes and necessities to those who had lost everything they owned to a fire."

"Yes, and Catarina's favorite thing to do was hand out stuffed animals to the children," BJ interjects.

"There was this one little girl, Julia. She was so sweet. I just fell in love with her. Thank you two so much for making a difference in this world. It's been what, sixteen years, and the lessons we learned are timeless. You guys have touched so many lives and helped so many."

"That's what I need to talk to you about," Angel turns to Dominic to address him directly.

BJ puts an end to their gathering, "It was really nice seeing you both. We have lots to do, and it sounds like you do too."

"Thanks again," Catarina says as she picks up Julie to leave.

"Take care and see you soon," Chief Morales bows to Princess Julie and smiles.

"What's up?" Dominic asks Angel.

"Well, you know we have always made a good team when we put our heads together. I mean, did you see that great-looking couple and their beautiful princess? We did that."

"Ok, so what's up?" Dominic repeats.

"Well, this feels like a Savory and Sweet 16 kind of day. Do you have time for lunch?"

"Sure. Meet you there."

# Chapter 15
# Angel's Plea

Angel arrives at the restaurant. Dominic has already gotten a table.

"Long time no see, Chief," Dominic laughs. "I like that. Can I call you Chief?"

"Sure, Your Honor."

"Ah, never mind, let's stick to Dominic and Angel. So, what's up?"

"Well, we answered a 911 call a few weeks ago," Angel explains. "It was an overdose found on the street, female, sixteen years old, with child, found out later that it's actually twins."

"We have surely seen some horrible things in our lifetime," Dominic murmurs.

"We administered Narcan, and her eyes opened wide. No! No! No! Let me go! she cried out as soon as she came to. Seeing her laying there like that, pleading to let her go," Angel pauses. "She was frantic. I stepped in to help, and her eyes caught mine," he pauses again, but this time for a little longer. "Well, I was able to calm her and she was transported to General Hospital."

"That's terrible," Dominic sympathizes. "But you said you need my help?"

"Yes. She was put on hold as a suicide attempt and admitted. This girl, Dominic, has had a rough life. Anyway, during therapy, it came out that it was not a suicide attempt. It was attempted murder."

"What?" Dominic asks, confused.

"She told everyone in group, including her counselor, that she did not want to kill herself, but she could not bear to bring children into this world. It is too cruel, and she is afraid for their future. You see, she claims that the foster father was going to take them away from her, and she could not allow that."

"How do you know all of this?" Dominic asks.

"The officer that responded to the call saw the arrest warrant come across his desk and contacted me. He had to go pick her up. She is in Juvie right now, but they are considering trying her as an adult."

Dominic sat and waited for more.

"I have visited her. There is just something about this case that has touched my heart," Angel made the sign of the cross. "She had filed for emancipation prior to this incident. It had not been granted yet, but I think this is why they may want to charge her as an adult for the attempted murder of her unborn babies."

"Can you get her in your courtroom? Can you look at her file and see if there is any way we can help her? This girl has had a rough life and needs help. I've looked into her eyes. She can be saved."

"I'll see what I can do," was Dominic's only response. "No promises."

"I'll take it," replies Angel with a slight sigh of relief. "Come on, I've got lots of quarters. Let's go shoot some hoops."

The men go to the basketball game, insert some quarters, and reminisce before heading back to work.

Dominic, as promised, studies the case prior to the young girl's court date. The girl's name is Diana Moksha. She has lived a very rough life. It was just as Angel had said. She was 16 years old and pregnant with twins. A bystander reported seeing her walking alone. He stated that she looked drunk. He called 911 upon seeing her fall down, losing consciousness. Paramedics report that it was actually an overdose. She was administered Narcan and brought to the nearest hospital.

This child, who had possibly tried to take her own life, had definitely, by her own account, tried to take the life of her unborn children and was now facing charges on two counts of feticide, the killing of an unborn child. A guilty verdict meant life in prison.

Dominic pulls all of Diana's juvenile and medical files. It was clear the system had failed this child. There was abuse at her home, possibly going back to infancy. She was abused mentally, physically, and sexually. Child Protective Services had been contacted several times, but the parents had covered their tracks. They moved around a lot and always took her to different doctors for her injuries to avoid suspicion. It wasn't until the age of thirteen that she was finally taken out of her home and placed in a foster home. Now, she is 16. She had filed for emancipation so she could live independently as an adult. The request was denied because she could not prove herself capable of financial independence.

Diana has appealed the ruling, but the appeal has yet to be heard. Dominic makes arrangements to handle the appeal for emancipation himself. If Angel feels she can be helped, he is all in. Dominic investigates ways that he can assist this young lady.

Angel continues to do his part by visiting Diana when allowed. She regrets her actions and speaks openly to Angel about her troubles. He encourages her to have faith and trust in the Lord. Jesus himself went through many hard times, but his faith never wavered.

Worries build, and weeks pass for Diana. She finds herself back in the courtroom for her emancipation appeal.

"Ms. Diana Moksha, can you please approach the bench with your counsel," Judge Dominic Baxter announces.

Diana and her court-appointed lawyer walk up to the bench. She keeps her head down as she walks. She is definitely pregnant, there is no denying it. The weeks she spent in the hospital and psychiatric unit had helped her get to a healthy pregnancy weight. The regular meals and vitamins had made her body flourish.

"Ms. Diana Moksha?" Judge Baxter questions her.

"Yes," she said as she continues looking down.

"There are legal ways to end a pregnancy, Ms. Moksha. Overdosing on the street at five months pregnant is not one of them."

"No," she spoke again with her head down.

"Look up at me when you speak," Judge Baxter insists.

She slowly raised her head. Her big brown eyes look at Dominic.

"Excuse me," Judge Baxter says, shaken by her gaze. He needs a minute. He looks at the file again. He had studied it front to back, knew everything about it, knew this young lady had been through the wringer, there was nothing more in that file to help him. He just was not ready for what he saw. No wonder Angel wanted him to take this case. Those eyes reached out and grabbed him. They touched his very soul. Angel must have noticed the same thing. Those eyes, he knew them.

Dominic composes himself, "I know this is your emancipation appeal and not your criminal case, but we do need to discuss your actions taken against the unborn fetuses."

"The babies?" she asks. "They not my babies," she says.

"Excuse me," Dominic responds.

"They not my babies," she repeats.

"I would like to meet with you two in my chamber. Take an hour, get a bite to eat, and meet me in my chambers at 2 pm," Judge Baxter banged his gavel and dismissed Ms. Moksha and her attorney. He proceeds to clear his load for the remainder of the day. Dominic is shaken. He enters his office and immediately calls Angel.

"What is this? Who is this you sent me? I do not understand what's going on."

"All I know is how I felt when I looked at her. It is the same feeling I had with Aidan and the same with your sister. We need to help her."

"How am I supposed to help her? She has to help herself. She is talking crazy. Says the babies aren't hers."

"But can't you give her a chance? She has paid dearly for the sins of her forefathers. Can't you see it? God is giving us another chance to help."

"The sins of our forefathers?" Dominic asks. "What does that even mean? She is facing life in prison. They want to try her as an adult. If I give her emancipation, she WILL be tried as an adult. It is a no-win situation."

"I know, that's why she needs you," Angel insists.

Dominic puts his head down, tries to compose himself, and awaits anxiously for 2 pm.

Exactly at 2 pm, there is a knock on his door.

"Come in," Judge Baxter calls out.

Diana and her counsel walk into his chambers.

"What did you mean when you said they were not your babies?" Dominic asks, wasting no time.

"These babies belong to my foster dad. He said that he would take them from me and teach them the ways of the world. I can't let that happen. I was trying to spare them," Diana cries out.

"I will do whatever it takes to protect them. I will suffer the fires of hell for my sins. I would rather be in hell and them in heaven. I know it was wrong, but I can't let my stepfather have them. Don't let him have these babies," Diana continues to cry out.

Suddenly, it clicks for Dominic. She does need our help. The system has failed her all of her life, and she doesn't want the same for the babies.

Diana sits down, looks up, and cries. "I am just so tired. I can't bring babies into this world. It's too cruel."

"Well, don't you fear Ms. Moksha, we are going to get you all the help you need. And your foster dad, what is his name? We will do a paternity test, and if the babies are his, he will spend his final years in prison."

"They are," she said. "I hadn't been out of the house to see anyone else. They're his. When Child Protective Services took me from my parents, I thought, things have got to get better. Nothing can be worse than what I was going through. Then, they moved me to my new place, and I learned it could always be worse."

"Well, Ms. Moksha, you are a few steps ahead of many people in understanding the world's ways. What you have experienced should never be. I wish I could take all the pain away, but I can't. What I can do is offer you a chance at a fresh start, a new life. It will not be easy, but nothing has been easy for you yet, and you have made it this far."

"I will do what I have to survive, but what I can't do is bring babies into this world for him," she cries. "It's too cruel."

"Oh, no!" Dominic reassures Diana. "If the babies are his, your stepfather will never get custody of them. I have a friend, let me tell you, his name is Angel, and I think he may be your guardian angel. He has asked that I look after you, and that is just what I intend to do."

"Their life can be beautiful with you in it. You have seen the worst of things, and you are still here. I have seen people with everything, with the world, their oysters, and they still are not happy. Some people have everything yet can give nothing. You have nothing, but something tells me you would give these children everything."

"I would, Judge Baxter. I would," she looks up. Her eyes, again, looked right through Dominic, into his soul and she felt a sense of peace and comfort, a comfort she had never experienced before.

"YOU are my angel," Diana whispers, "You are my angel."

After a few formalities, phone calls, and signatures, Diana and her counsel leave. Dominic works feverishly to get all the proper channels and pieces involved. The wheels are in motion. A petition that

Diana's emancipation request be considered and her criminal charges possibly waived is filed.

Of course, there is a lot of legal jargon and requirements, but it looks promising if Diana attends and fulfills the requirements of a treatment program. Dominic gets the authorities involved to investigate the stepfather and gets a social worker to help make arrangements for long-term therapy and living arrangements for Diana.

The wheels are in motion. Dominic is exhausted and unsettled. He calls Angel, and they meet for dinner at their go-to, Savory and Sweet 16.

"That girl," Dominic says to Angel. "It is a horrible situation, and she has a long way to recover. I'm glad you asked me to get involved."

"There is just something about her," they say simultaneously.

"It's the eyes," Dominic states.

"I feel it, too," Angel agrees.

"Thanks again for reaching out and giving me the chance to make a difference. You are a good man, Angel Morales."

"Ah, don't get all mushy on me now. Come on, I have some quarters."

# Chapter 16
# Diana

"I am Diana Moksha, and I am a survivor," I say in the strongest voice I can muster. I then sit down and hang my head. I don't feel much like a survivor. I do not feel worthy of being here and why, why have Chief Morales and Judge Baxter taken such interest in me? Why does anyone care?

"I am Diana Moksha, and I am a survivor," I must say this twice a day. It is part of the counseling program here at the maternity home I have been placed in. We meet twice a week, sit around in a circle, and share. I look around and see other women, some my age, some younger, some older. Most of us are pregnant, but a few have already given birth. The home has a sitter for the babies so that the mothers can still attend. I sit and listen to the stories these women tell and feel like I should not speak. I do not deserve their sympathy.

I have always been a burden to someone. Once I got pregnant, I didn't have it so bad. I had it easy, yet I tried to destroy it. Some of the women had to fight for their lives. They were beaten on a daily basis, yet still protected their child. Once I got pregnant, no one hit me anymore, yet I tried to end it. I am only a survivor because I screwed up. Someone found me and called 911.

"You say you are a survivor, and you are Diana," says Mrs. Munn, "but then you sit down and hang your head. You are worthy and deserve to be healthy, happy, and confident. But for some reason, I do not think you believe it."

"What makes you happy, Mrs. Munn?" I ask.

"Well, you guys do," she replies. "Your success is what makes me happy. Helping you guys. I was once where you were, you know."

"What helped you change your life," I ask.

"Believe it or not, it was a quote I read written by the Dalai Lama. 'It is under the greatest adversity that there exists the greatest potential for doing good, both for oneself and others.' This is what turned my life around. I chose to use my trauma to strengthen myself and grow productively. When I see others suffering, I am determined to help. I have always heard it is better to give than to receive, and now I understand. You all, your success, makes me happy," Mrs. Munn says and smiles while looking around.

I noticed she looked at each person in the circle. She really meant what she was saying. She made it all the way back around to me.

"What do you want to do with your life, Diana?" Mrs. Munn inquires.

"I just want to give these babies a good life."

"Then, that is what you will do," she assures me.

"I hear people talk, I see the news," I answer back. "They think I am not good enough. That they should take these babies away from me..." I pause, hang my head, and sniffle.

"But what?" Mrs. Munn prods.

"It makes me sick to think of someone else having them. How would I protect them? What if they take them away from me because of my overdose? I was trying to protect them! I know it was wrong, but I did not know what else to do." I can hear the pitch of my voice increase.

"Girl, no one can take your babies," a young girl says with attitude.

"You fight to keep them!" another woman interjects.

Mrs. Munn settles the room, "Let's look at some facts. You were placed here, correct?"

"Yes."

"Didn't that judge order a paternity check and have your foster parent arrested?"

"Yes."

"Haven't you been taking advantage of all our resources such as our pregnancy, childbirth, parenting classes, and job training?"

"Yes."

"Then, it looks like you are on the right track. You must use your experiences to grow stronger and more confident. Remember, sometimes great adversity allows for the greatest potential for doing good, both for oneself and others, for you and your babies," Mrs. Munn reassures me.

"I know I can survive. I have survived this long, but I want more for my children. I want them to thrive."

"You have to want to thrive for yourself, too, and through that, you will create a world where your children can thrive. Keep putting in the work."

And from that day on, that's exactly what I did.

"I am Diana Moksha, a survivor who is going to thrive," I tell myself every night, looking in the mirror. I don't always believe it, but I am willing to put in the work.

It's been four months since my overdose. I am a week and a half from my due date. I have to work on forgiving myself. I know it was a terrible thing to do, but the intention behind it was good, just misdirected.

Tuesday morning arrives, and I waddle to the shower. I let the warm water run down my aching back and across my oversized belly. I think about the babies and if they can feel the sensation of the water. One day, they will be playing in the sprinkler. I close my eyes and imagine. I used to daydream all the time, but those seemed like fantasies. These thoughts, I can make them come true.

I finish showering and get ready to go. I have my court-mandated therapy session every Tuesday, and every Tuesday, Judge Baxter picks me up from my group home and drives me to my session. We visit a little on the ride, and conversation comes fairly naturally and easily. I don't quite understand why he is so kind to me and why he drives me to therapy every week, although I am very grateful. Maybe it's his duty to make sure I attend. I'm not sure. It doesn't seem right to me, but what do I know?

"Thanks for the ride. I will see you next week."

I struggle to get out of his car. This belly is getting bigger, and time is short. My due date is fast approaching.

Judge Baxter stops me, "Look, I know you usually manage your own ride home, but I was wondering if you would like to go with me and Chief Morales to lunch today. I know he would love to see you. He asks about you often."

"Ummm, sure," I say. "I have been having really long sessions, at least two hours. We are doing hypnotherapy or hypnotic regression. My therapist puts me in, like, a trance, and it is supposed to help me remember stuff that is 'buried deep inside and not available to my conscious mind,'" I quote what was told to me.

"Some people even explore past lives. I think that is so cool. My counselor says that it may help me get better faster. I don't remember what happened during the regression sessions. I just sit there, relax and seem to fall asleep. But she says that I talk to her about things. Kinda weird. Seems strange to me. Spoooooky huh? Ooooooooohhh," I try to make the sound of a ghost.

We both laugh a little.

"We do regular talk therapy, too. Not sure which is helping more, but I am feeling better."

"That's great news. Well, if you are up for lunch, I will pick you up in a couple of hours," Dominic confirms.

"Sure," I smile and head into the office.

Why, I wonder again, why is he so nice to me and why does that fire chief care about me? I bring the question up to my therapist.

We talk about it for a little bit, and of course, she turns it around and wants to know why it bothers me. She assures me there are good people in the world, and I deserve every bit of kindness that comes my way. She, of course, has already questioned me about his intent and has apparently spoken with him too. She assures me that he is on the up and up and is big into volunteering and helping others. She also tells me about his sister who killed herself when he was young.

"Maybe it helps him feel good that he can help you since he was never able to help his sister," she explains. "In fact, he and Chief Morales have created two very successful non-profit organizations that focus on giving people opportunities to volunteer and help others."

"Well, maybe one day I will be able to return the favor and get involved. Right now, I need to learn to take care of myself so that I can take care of these two."

I rub my big belly and can feel them kick.

"It's like they are excited that I am on the right track. I love them so much already."

My therapist and I talk for about an hour before we begin the regression. She always likes to go over what has happened, how I am handling it, and whether I remember anything from the last session I want to discuss. I usually don't remember anything, but I like it. It makes me relaxed.

"One day, you may remember what you talked to me about while regressed, or you may never. Sometimes things may appear in your conscious memory as a flash. You may have what some people refer to as déjà vu. If this ever happens and you need me, you can always call. If you feel the session relaxes you, we will continue."

She talks me through the regression, and I wake feeling refreshed. We end the session by setting up my goals for the week and reviewing my long-term goals of living as a strong, independent single mother.

"I'm gonna have my own little apartment. I'll paint the babies' rooms bright yellow and fill them with butterflies and a big beautiful rainbow."

"That sounds really great," she says to me as I leave my session.

I exit the building and see Judge Baxter waiting for me. I am really hungry and am excited to be going to lunch. I felt a little strange about it when he first asked, but since my session, I feel much more relaxed and look forward to seeing Chief Morales. I do not know that I ever officially thanked him for all he has done for me.

Judge Baxter opens the car door and closes it after I manage to squeeze in. We drive to what he describes as their favorite place to eat, Savory and Sweet 16, food and fun. We walk in and see Chief Morales sitting in a booth.

"Over here," he says. "We normally sit at a high table, but I didn't think that was the best idea for today," he says as he looks at my big belly. I look around and notice the basketball theme.

"Fit right in with my belly. Looks like I'm carrying a whole team in here," I joke.

"You look great," Chief Morales says.

"Thanks, been feeling much better too, thanks to you two. You saved our lives, mine and my babies. I am so grateful. How can I ever repay you?" I ask and cry a tear.

"You just live the best life you can," they both agree.

We eat, laugh, and visit. I ask about the programs they have created, DO and Youth on Fire, and I see their eyes light up. Maybe it is better to give than to receive. I think of what Mrs. Munn said to me. This feels good. It feels real. A warmth runs through me. I don't think I have ever felt this before. I can see how they thrive from helping others. Maybe one day I can pay it forward.

After we placed our order, Dominic said, "Ok, we have another tradition. I always have to show him up at the basketball game. Do you want to shoot some?"

"Oh no," I laugh, "you two go ahead. I'll just sit here and watch."

The two of them get up and head over to the arcade game. They put their money in and start shooting with a frenzy. Chief Morales wins the first game. He celebrates and laughs.

It's fun to watch the two of them and hear them rib each other.

"I let you win. I can beat you with my eyes closed," Judge Baxter says and puts more quarters in the machine.

"Stay with me," Chief Morales tells him. "You have so much to learn. We aren't finished here yet."

Whoa, déjà vu. Things start moving in slow motion. I see Dominic close his eyes, shoot and score. He then proceeds to do some weird little dance moves. Both men start laughing, but it's all still in slow motion. The sound of their laughter is dragging. Things aren't so fun for me. Visions start flashing in my mind. They are flashing by so quickly. It's Dom and Angel. I see flashes of their younger selves. I am not feeling so well.

Suddenly, my stomach contracts. I am not sure what is happening.

"Oh," I scream.

A waitress passing by notices me and calls for help.

Dom and Angel come to my rescue. They load me in the car and drive me to the hospital. My contractions are getting stronger. The pain they cause pulls me out of my trancelike state and into reality, a very scary reality of this is it. They are coming. My babies are coming.

I am rushed into the hospital and taken to labor and delivery. I am immediately examined by my obstetrician and am told it won't be long now and everything looks great.

"I know. I can see more clearly now. I understand," I blubber out to the doctor.

"You are doing great," the nurse assures me. "Keep breathing."

"Are Dom and Angel here?" I ask.

"You mean Judge Baxter and Chief Morales? Yes, they are right outside."

"Yes, of course, Judge Baxter and Chief Morales. Knowing they are there will help me through my labor. I now know I am not alone and that I will always have help. They are a part of my new family."

Hours pass, and I deliver a beautiful baby girl, all tiny and wrinkly, and then a beautiful baby boy. They are so perfect, perfect in every way. I hold both babies, one in each arm. I have never known a love so great. Their eyes look at me, and I know they are mine, and I am theirs. I will forever protect and care for them. I cannot wait to fulfill my destiny to live a full and happy life. I can't even describe the love I feel. They are so innocent and pure.

# Surviving Sixteen

"There are two very anxious men out here waiting to see you," a nurse says as she enters my room.

"Please, tell them to come in."

Dominic and Angel come into the room, grinning from ear to ear.

"Look at you," Dominic says so sweetly.

"They are beautiful, a boy and a girl."

"They are perfect," I beam.

"We won't stay long. We know you need your rest," they say. "We are just happy to know that you and the babies are all doing well."

"Can you come back tomorrow? You have helped me so much, I want you to be a part of their lives, part of our family. You two have taught me what it means to care for someone. I don't need an answer now, but if you can consider," I pause. With a little hesitation in my voice I continue, "I'd like for you each to be a Godparent."

Angel and Dominic look at one another and tear up.

"We would love that," Angel says.

"It would be an honor," added Dominic.

"Have you named those beautiful babies yet?" Angel asks.

"Not yet, I need to look at them, hold them for a while, feel their essence. It will come to me."

"We are honored to know you and to be part of your family," says Dominic, "but we must go and let you get some rest."

"Thanks again for everything, guys. Will I see you soon?"

"Of course," they say, "you couldn't keep us away. We will come by tomorrow."

The two proud Godparents walk away as the nurse walks in.

"I need to take the babies to the nursery for a little bit, and you need some rest."

"As long as you promise to bring them back."

I take a long look at my beautiful babies and kiss their heads before she takes them.

"Can I get a pen and something to write on?"

"Sure, but you need to rest while you can," my nurse reiterates.

"And two envelopes, please," I plea.

The nurse returns with a pen, paper, and two envelopes. I want to write two letters, one to Angel and one to Dominic. There is so much I want to say to them.

Before I begin writing, my thoughts go back to my beautiful newborns. I have yet to name them. I think, but nothing comes to me. I write down my own name. I begin mixing the letters up and there are two perfect names.

I now carefully pen my letters to Angel and Dom and seal them in their envelopes. I tell the nurse I expect them to visit the next day and would like them to read the letters before entering my room. She agrees and takes the letters. I now rest and enjoy the evening with my babies, telling them of the beautiful future that we have in store.

# Chapter 17
# The Letters

The next day arrives, the sun is shining, and a rainbow appears across the sky. Everything is looking brighter. I am so grateful to be alive and have an opportunity to take the bull by the horns. Life is what you make it, and I intend to make it great.

I am feeling tired, but I couldn't be happier. I just finished nursing my two beautiful babies. When I look up, I see Angel has arrived first. He is given his letter.

*Dear Chief Morales,*

*I know you. You are a man of God. You are an angel sent from heaven to earth. You are here to do God's work. Your unwavering faith has saved so many souls and your dedication to your job, countless lives. Every life you touch touches someone else. You will never know your reach. Your rewards will be great.*

*Love,*
*Diana*

Angel enters the room with tears in his eyes.

"You are wise beyond your years, young lady. I am touched by your words, and I pray that I have spread God's goodness as much as you have given me credit."

He wipes a tear from his face.

"Now, I think we need to come up with a better name than Chief Morales."

"Ok," I reply and smile. "I thought about Chief Angel, but that's a little much."

"Oh, very funny, how about just Angel?"

"Sounds perfect!"

I look up and see out of my hospital room, Angel had left the door open a crack. It is Dominic. He has arrived and the nurse has given him his envelope. His back is to us, but I can tell he is opening the letter. He begins to read. I think of the words I have written and cry a single tear.

**Dom,**

*I know you. I have always known you. You are the one who always looks out for others. You teach that life can become what you make it.*

Dominic pauses, closing his eyes. He sees Diana's familiar brown eyes in Nadia's. Nadia is laughing at Dominic's younger self, dancing the floss and playing chase. He remembers helping Nadia with the dishes. He is slightly confused but continues.

*I have learned that death is not an escape. Choosing death only causes more pain. I'm sorry for the hurt I caused. I am so sorry.*

Dominic squeezes his eyes shut. Those deep brown eyes that have haunted him. He sees it now. The eyes remain, but the faces change. They belong to them all, first Nadia, then Aidan, and finally, Diana. Dominic collapses to his knees in disbelief.

*Give it time. Sometimes, things are difficult, and lessons take a while to understand.*

Dominic suddenly recalls Aidan's nametag, reflecting Nadia's name in the window and Aiden calling him Dom in such a familiar way. Now, Diana is asking him to be the Godfather of her children. He feels their spirit.

*You are the one! You have helped me realize that life is to be given to others, not taken away. Life is to be lived and felt fully, and it is in giving that we receive. I want to thank you, thank you for sticking with me and giving me everlasting life.*

Dominic, kneeling on the ground, begins to sob. Those brown eyes pierce into him and fill his soul. He feels more complete.

*I am no longer in need of anything and, therefore, willingly and knowingly give all of myself to my wonderful children. Thank you for always being a part of our world. I look forward to our future.*

*Love Always and Forever,*

*Diana and My Babies,*

*Aidan & Nadia*

# **About The Author**

Tina Prima Knaps is a dynamic individual whose life experiences have fueled her passion for storytelling. A retired teacher and coach, she understands the power of mentorship, perseverance, and teamwork. As a former Tulane University Volleyball player, she learned the value of discipline, dedication, and resilience. Married with two daughters, Tina draws inspiration from her family by exploring themes of love, loss, and redemption in her writing. A survivor of a suicide attempt and chronic health issues, she brings a unique perspective to her work, infusing her narratives with authenticity, empathy, and hope. Through her writing, Tina Knaps seeks to inspire others to overcome adversity and find strength in the face of challenges.

# Mental Health Resources

Today, we have immediate access to mental health support through helplines, online therapy, apps, and support groups. Educational resources, creative therapy, and crisis services are readily available. The cultural dialogue around mental health has transformed, making support accessible and stigma-free. You're not alone; help is here.

**The Trevor Project:**

For LGBTQ youth, offering crisis intervention and suicide prevention services. Call 1-866-488-7386, text START to 678678, or chat online.

**Teen Line:**

Teen-to-teen support, call 800-852-8336 or text TEEN to 839863 for help.

**Your Life Your Voice**:

For youth, offers free, confidential support 24/7. Call 1-800-448-3000 or text "VOICE" to 20121.

**Specialized Services: Postpartum Support International (PSI):**

Support for emotional changes during and after pregnancy, call 1-800-944-4PPD (4773).

## 988 Suicide & Crisis Lifeline:

Call or Text 988 for immediate help. This service provides 24/7 support for anyone experiencing a mental health crisis or suicidal thoughts.

## Crisis Text Line:

Text "HOME" to 741741 for free, 24/7 crisis support via text message.

## Substance Abuse and Mental Health Services Administration (SAMHSA):

National Helpline: 1-800-662-HELP (4357) offers free, confidential 24/7 treatment referral and information service.

## National Alliance on Mental Illness (NAMI):

NAMI Helpline: 1-800-950-NAMI (6264) or email helpline@nami.org (mailto:helpline@nami.org). Offers information, resources, and support.

# **Pact For Survival**

This pact serves as a personal reminder and promise to oneself to navigate through life's trials with resilience and determination.

I, [Your Name], hereby pledge:

To seek help when I feel overwhelmed or in despair.

To engage with mental health resources available to me.

To communicate openly with those who care about me.

To prioritize self-care and well-being.

To remember that no matter the challenge, there is always a way forward.

I commit to doing whatever I can to survive, to thrive, and to embrace life's journey, no matter how difficult it may seem.

Signed: [Your Signature] [Date]

# Letter Of Commitment To Ask For Help Before Harming Oneself

Dear [Recipient's Name]

I am writing this letter to you as a personal vow and a promise to myself. Life has its challenges, and at times, can feel overwhelming, leading to thoughts that might not be in my best interest. I want you to know that I am making a commitment to change how I handle those moments of despair or distress.

I hereby vow to seek help before ever considering harming myself. I understand that there are people who care about me, resources available to support me, and professionals who can guide me through any dark times. I pledge to:

- Reach out to friends, family, or trusted individuals when I feel overwhelmed or distressed.
- Contact a mental health professional or use helpline services when I need immediate support.
- Engage in activities or practices that have previously helped me cope with stress or negative emotions.
- Remind myself that my feelings, no matter how intense, are temporary and that there are always other solutions to my problems.

I recognize that asking for help is not a sign of weakness but an act of strength and self-care. I promise to honor this commitment by:

- Keeping a list of emergency contacts easily accessible.
- Regularly attending counseling or therapy sessions, even when I feel "okay."
- Participating in support groups or community activities that foster a sense of belonging and support.
- Educating myself and those around me about mental health, reducing stigma, and ensuring we all know how to support each other.

I know that this journey might not always be easy, but with your encouragement and my commitment, I believe I can navigate through the toughest of times.

Thank you for being part of my life, for listening when I need to talk, and for being there when I need support. I value our relationship, and I'm looking forward to continuing to grow and heal, with your help and the help of others.

With sincere gratitude and commitment,

[Your Name]

www.ingramcontent.com/pod-product-compliance
Lightning Source LLC
LaVergne TN
LVHW021816060526
838201LV00058B/3411